Critical Muslim 11

Syria

Editors: Ziauddin Sardar and Robin Yassin-Kassab

Deputy Editor: Samia Rahman

Senior Editors: Aamer Hussein, Hassan Mahamdallie, Ehsan Masood, Ebrahim Moosa

Publisher: Michael Dwyer

Managing Editor (Hurst Publishers): Daisy Leitch

Cover Design: Fatima Jamadar

Associate Editors: Alev Adil, Nazry Bahrawi, Merryl Wyn Davies, Abdulwahhab El-Affendi, Marilyn Hacker, Nader Hashemi, Vinay Lal, Iftikhar Malik, Shanon Shah, Boyd Tonkin

International Advisory Board: Waqar Ahmad, Karen Armstrong, William Dalrymple, Farid Esack, Anwar Ibrahim, Robert Irwin, Bruce Lawrence, Ashis Nandy, Ruth Padel, Bhikhu Parekh, Barnaby Rogerson, Malise Ruthven

Critical Muslim is published quarterly by C. Hurst & Co. (Publishers) Ltd. on behalf of and in conjunction with Critical Muslim Ltd. and the Muslim Institute, London.

All correspondence to Muslim Institute, CAN Mezzanine, 49-51 East Road, London N1 6AH, United Kingdom

e-mail for editorial: editorial@criticalmuslim.com

C. Hurst & Co. (Publishers) Ltd.,41 Great Russell Street, London WC1B 3PL

ISBN: 978-1-84904-451-6 ISSN: 2048-8475

To subscribe or place an order by credit/debit card or cheque (pound sterling only) please contact Kathleen May at the Hurst address above or e-mail kathleen@hurstpub.co.uk

Tel: 020 7255 2201

A one year subscription, inclusive of postage (four issues), costs £50 (UK), £65 (Europe) and £75 (rest of the world).

The British Museum

Discover the Islamic World

From early scientific instruments to contemporary art, explore how Islam has shaped our world through objects for centuries

Great Russell Street,
London WC1B 3DG
⊖ Tottenham Court Road,
Holborn, Russell Square
britishmuseum.org

Mosque lamp. Enamelled glass.
Syria, c. AD 1330–1345.

HALAL FOOD FOUNDATION

Halal Is Much More Than Food

The Halal Food Foundation (HFF) is a registered charity that aims to make the concept of halal more accessible and mainstream. We want people to know that halal does not just pertain to food – halal is a lifestyle.

The Foundation pursues its goals through downloadable resources, events, social networking, school visits, pursuing and funding scientific research on issues of food and health, and its monthly newsletter. We work for the community and aim at the gradual formation of a consumer association. We aim to educate and inform; and are fast becoming the first port of call on queries about halal issues. We do not talk at people, we listen to them.

If you have any queries, comments, ideas, or would just like to voice your opinion - please get in contact with us.

Halal Food Foundation

109 Fulham Palace Road,
Hammersmith, London, W6 8JA
Charity number: 1139457
Website: www.halalfoodfoundation.co.uk
E-mail: info@halalfoodfoundation.co.uk

 @HFF_UK

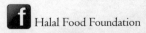 Halal Food Foundation

The Barbary Figs

by

Rashid Boudjedra

Translated by
André Naffis-Sahely

RASHID AND OMAR are cousins who find themselves side by side on a flight from Algiers to Constantine. During the hour-long journey, the pair will exhume their past, their boyhood in French Algeria during the 1940s and their teenage years fighting in the bush during the revolution. Rashid, the narrator, has always resented Omar, who despite all his worldly successes, has been on the run from the ghosts of his past, ghosts that Rashid has set himself the task of exorcising. Rashid peppers his account with chilling episodes from Algerian history, from the savageries of the French invasion in the 1830s, to the repressive regime that is in place today.

RASHID BOUDJEDRA has routinely been called one of North Africa's leading writers since his debut, *La Répudiation*, was published in 1969, earning the author the first of many fatwas. While he wrote his first six novels in French, Boudjedra switched to Arabic in 1982 and wrote another six novels in the language before returning to French in 1994. *The Barbary Figs* was awarded the Prix du Roman Arabe 2010.

CM11

July–September 2014

CONTENTS

SYRIA

ARTS AND LETTERS

Homs – the city that was © Ross Burns

Subscribe to Critical Muslim

Now in its second year, *Critical Muslim* is the only publication of its kind, giving voice to the diversity and plurality of Muslim reporting, creative writing, poetry and scholarship.

Subscribe now to receive each issue of Critical Muslim direct to your door and save money on the cover price of each issue.

Subscriptions are available at the following prices, inclusive of postage. Subscribe for two years and save 10%!

	ONE YEAR (4 Issues)	TWO YEARS (8 Issues)
UK	£50	£90
Europe	£65	£117
Rest of World	£75	£135

TO SUBSCRIBE:

CRITICALMUSLIM.HURSTPUBLISHERS.COM

41 GREAT RUSSELL ST, LONDON WC1B 3PL
WWW.HURSTPUBLISHERS.COM
WWW.FBOOK.COM/HURSTPUBLISHERS
020 7255 2201

SYRIA

THE ROOTS OF THE SYRIAN CRISIS

Peter Clark

In the 1890s a twenty-year-old Englishman was in the Umayyad Mosque in Damascus. He had been travelling for a year in Palestine and Syria and was deeply affected by all he saw. He told an elderly official of the mosque that he wanted to embrace Islam. The old man advised against such a move. 'Wait till you are older,' the old man said, 'and have seen again your native land. You are alone among us . . . God knows how I should feel if any Christian teacher dealt with a son of mine otherwise than as I now deal with you.'

Twenty years later that young man did embrace Islam. He was Marmaduke Pickthall, and he went on to render the Holy Qur'an into English, deliver *khutba*s at mosques in London, and was finally buried at the Muslim cemetery at Brookwood.

Twenty years before Pickthall's first visit to Damascus, another very different British traveller came to that city. He was between visits to Najd in the Arabian Peninsula. Charles Montagu Doughty later wrote an account of his travels in *Arabia Deserta*. That book opens with an encounter between Doughty and a Damascus friend:

A new voice hailed me of an old friend when, first returned from the Peninsula, I paced again in that long street which is called Straight; and suddenly taking me wondering by the hand 'Tell me (said he), since thou art here again in the peace and assurance of Ullah, and whilst we walk, as in the former years, toward the new blossoming orchards, full of the sweet spring as the garden of God, what moved thee, or how couldst thou take such journeys into the fanatic Arabia?'

These two testimonies of the century before last bear witness to a tradition of openness and inclusiveness in Syria, of a legacy of accepting religious difference. The Muslims, Christians and Jews of Syria were sure of their faith. Syria in general and Damascus in particular were important to each of the Abrahamic religions. Indeed local legends maintained that the first murder, Cain's slaying of Abel, was committed on Jabal Qasiyun overlooking the city. His tomb, forty kilometres to the west, is guarded by Druze and is a place on the Iranian pilgrimage route. Another legend claims that the second coming of Jesus will take place in Damascus. He will descend from the Isa minaret of the Umayyad Mosque. The Prophet Muhammad himself is believed to have approached Damascus, and his footprint was preserved to the south of the city in the suburb, Qadam.

This plurality – and many more examples could be cited – demonstrates that the current civil war, where all sorts of unbelievable atrocities are being committed daily, often in religion's name, is an aberration of Syrian history. The traditions of openness harmonise with the practice of Syrians themselves and the observations of countless visitors.

What has gone wrong?

In the next few pages I would like to tease out the reasons for the openness. I wish to show how it was reflected in the practice of the Ottomans, who controlled Syria for four hundred years until 1918. I will show how the balance between communities was undermined under the French Mandate of 1920–46, with consequences neither the French nor anybody else planned or were able to predict. I will touch on the rise of the Alawites to political prominence over the last seventy years, reaching its peak in the last ten. I will then assess the strengths and failings of the regimes of the Assads, father and son, compare the political skills of the two, and consider how the present ghastly situation has been arrived at.

At present over a tenth of the population are refugees in neighbouring countries. In total, over forty per cent of Syrians have been displaced. Tom Hill's encounters with refugee children – part of a lost generation who have missed years of education – in the Atmeh camp in northern Syria, provide a flavour of the tragedy. Thousands of others who have foreign passports, or who have friends, family or connections elsewhere, have emigrated. Meanwhile the Assad regime seems to be in control of only parts of the country and certainly not all of the major cities. Other areas are controlled by organised opposition groups, but many parts of the north and centre are under the control of perhaps hundreds of small groups. Sometimes it seems as if local warlords are controlling a village, a quarter of a town, perhaps just a block of flats. The government has been in possession of most of the heavy weaponry, and unprecedented havoc has been wreaked on residential areas believed to have sheltered opponents of the regime. The Free Syrian Army, a loose association of rebel forces commanded by defected army officers, has been eclipsed by the Islamic Front and more extreme Islamist militias. Sam Hamad, in his essay on the armed opposition, shows how 'the lack of material support for the moderate rebels has led to the over-representation on the battlefield of forces that are not necessarily ideologically popular'.

The idea of Syria goes back to classical times. It is certainly true that Syria has been a geographical term without any continuity as a political concept – but the same was true of most parts of the world before the concept of the nation-state. There has been a cultural continuity for thousands of years, leaving an archaeological heritage that is second to none, as archaeologist and former Australian diplomat in Damascus Ross Burns argues in his essay on the effects of war on the country's heritage, and what will need to be done to save what remains when the guns fall silent. Although Syria was part of the Greco-Roman world for a thousand years, from the conquests of Alexander in the fourth century BCE to the Islamic conquests of the seventh century CE, the people of geographical Syria were never culturally and linguistically submerged in the way that southern Europe was. There was a continuity of the Semitic languages – Aramaic the most widely used – that had been the means of communication before the classical conquests.

There were also three other Syrian characteristics that have prevailed to the present day: commercialism, migration and religion. Syria has always traded, and the people of the country were known as keen traders over two thousand years ago. And Syrians have always been on the move. Sometimes it went with the commercialism, but there were soldiers from Palmyra on Hadrian's Wall when England was a Roman colony. Syrians became Roman emperors and the mothers of emperors. Syrians became popes of Rome. Syrians provided the Byzantine Empire with traders and craftsmen. Until very recently, Aleppo's ancient textile industry continued to supply European markets – Malu Halasa's essay on 'the Bra in Aleppo' opens a window on this world presently suspended by bombs.

The third feature of Syria has been a strong religious tradition. The early history and development of the three Abrahamic religions have been linked to the land of Syria. Intense religious beliefs have nurtured strong loyalties to individuals and to diverse confessions. Where there has been persecution organised by authorities and practised in the cities, people have migrated to sanctuaries away from the urban areas. So Maronites, Druze, Alawis and Ismailis moved to the mountains. Orthodox Christians managed better under Muslim rulers. There were always significant Orthodox and other Christian communities in the cities, which were generally controlled by Sunni Muslims.

Just as a Syrian authenticity reasserted itself after Greco-Roman times, so it was little affected by the onslaught of the Crusades from the eleventh to thirteenth centuries CE. Outsiders, Ayoubids and Mamlukes, were able to overcome the plains and occupy the cities, wield authority and impose taxation from these bases, but usually had to negotiate with the commercial and religious families of Damascus and Aleppo and other cities for funds and legitimacy.

Such was the historical background to the four hundred years of Ottoman rule, the longest continuous rule of any one authority in Syria's history since the Islamic conquests. Ottoman rule in Syria was inclusive and generally (but not always) relaxed; insofar as there was a public policy it was that all people were allowed to co-exist under the rule of the Sultan. The diverse communities were seen not as minorities but as elements (*anāsīr*) of society. Different confessions had their own roles, although there was also the notion that each religious community existed as a separate state within the nation state, with their leaders held responsible for raising taxes and administering personal legal issues. In actual fact, different social classes of different religious communities shared values and spaces regardless (to a great extent) of their confession. It was only when there was a disequilibrium in the balance of different communities that the system broke down. In the early nineteenth century, Maronites in Lebanon migrated to the cities and prospered. This upset in the balance of power and wealth distribution led to the riots of 1860, after which the Ottoman government intervened to re-establish balance. The Lebanese civil war of 1975–90 can be seen as having a similar cause. The balance of communities became skewed by first, an influx of (Sunni) Palestinian refugees, then by the social and demographic emergence of Shi'ite communities.

At the beginning of the twentieth century Greater Syria had a diverse population under an Ottoman hegemony. Under Sultan Abdulhamid II, who ruled from 1876 to 1909, the Ottoman authorities asserted their rule with a series of measures: larger garrisons, better communications, the cult of the Sultan, improved education. The reforms owed more to the concept of a stronger state than to the notion of a liberal civil society – more Metternich than John Stuart Mill. The emphasis on Ottoman authority was manifested in the new schools where Turkish became the medium of education just as it was for law and government. This clashed with a nineteenth-century revival of Arab interest in the Arab cultural heritage.

Arab society before 1914 was not totally alienated from the Ottoman capital. Many Syrians did well in Istanbul. The *dawla* or *devlet* – the 'state' – commanded and received deference. Syrians like 'Izz al-Din al-'Abid were at the heart of power and influence at Yildiz Palace under Sultan Abdulhamid. Part of the legitimacy of the Ottoman Empire, especially in the Arab lands of the Levant, was based on its patronage of religious institutions and practices, and above all, the pilgrimage. In the first century of Ottoman rule, the chain of khans, staging posts, from Istanbul to the Hijaz, were constructed or renovated. Damascus was the starting point of one of the annual pilgrimage processions to the Holy Land. Muslims from Anatolia, the Ottoman capital, Bosnia, Transcaucasia, and Central Asia gathered in Damascus – stimulating the city's trade – and set off on the journey, two months there and two months back. An Ottoman-appointed official was in charge. Sometimes women of the Imperial Ottoman family (but, oddly, never the Sultan himself) accompanied the caravan to Mecca.

In the centre of Damascus stands a column that was erected between 1900 and 1908 to commemorate the linking of Istanbul, Damascus and Mecca by telegraph. Under Sultan Abdulhamid the project of the Hijaz Railway was launched; it was completed under his successors and brought prosperity to his city. The Damascene 'Izzat al-Din al-'Abid was instrumental in its promotion.

But the cooperation was threatened by the cultural policies of Istanbul, especially by the consciously *Turkish* Young Turks after 1908. When the Ottoman Empire imploded under the pressure of the First World War, the divergence between Syria and the capital increased. The local governor was deeply suspicious of Arab consciousness and nationalist activity, as a result of which many young men of the leading families of Greater Syria were symbolically hanged in the main squares of Damascus and Beirut. Syria was shattered politically, a situation exacerbated by famine at the end of the war.

The Great Powers decided on the fate of Syria. There were conflicting commitments, but by 1920 the French were awarded a Mandate to administer Syria and Lebanon, ostensibly in the interests of the country.

The French ran Syria for twenty-six years. They were deeply suspicious of the men from the families that had been effectively running the country during the Ottoman centuries. They were an official land-owning class who dominated society in Damascus and Aleppo, and to a lesser extent in Hama and Homs. Some of the families based their legitimacy on religious authority, taking revenues from *waqf* property (property donated by Muslims for religious or charitable purposes) and holding religious offices. But the French were unhappy with the Arab nationalist rhetoric of the Sunni Muslims, which they feared could undermine their control of the French Empire in North Africa. During the Mandate years the French divided and ruled. They established separate statelets for the Alawites, based in Lattakia, and the Druze, based in Suwaida, as well as another statelet in north-east Syria. Lebanon was also administered separately – a detachment that ultimately led to Lebanon becoming a distinct country. The French built up a local army based on the minorities that hailed from areas far from the cities. The urban Sunni families had tended not to send their sons into the Ottoman army anyway. So the French Mandate armies were largely composed of Alawites, Ismailis and Sunni Muslims from poorer, more rural parts of Syria. Christians and Armenians were also disproportionately represented among the French recruits. These forces, sometimes supplemented by soldiers from other French possessions, were used to suppress popular uprisings in the country. Meanwhile at the political level, negotiations for greater political autonomy were conducted with the political families of the big cities. These negotiations ultimately led, not without setbacks, to independence in 1946.

In the first twenty years after independence, governments were often dominated by individuals from or linked to the old city families. But from 1949 a series of military coups interrupted a pattern of politics that was not totally dissimilar to governance under the Ottomans. The military coups were part of a world phenomenon outside Europe in the decades after the Second World War. As elsewhere, the language of politics was nationalist and increasingly socialist. As we have seen, the Syrian army was disproportionately manned by non-Sunni Muslims. In particular the Alawites were moving up the hierarchy of the armed forces.

The Alawites were a dissident Shi'ite Muslim community, but their beliefs were, for political purposes, less significant than their role in Syrian society. For centuries they had been a marginalised community, with little clout in social and economic terms. Outside Lattakia, there were no large Alawite communities that made any impact on the politics of Aleppo or Damascus. They inhabited the mountains above the Mediterranean coast and, economically, were largely self-contained. Many of the men migrated seasonally to work on the estates of the Sunni notables, and many of the young women were often appallingly treated as house servants in the major cities.

Recruitment into the army meant a substantial exodus of Alawites from their homelands to the rest of the country. Their isolation ended.

Immediately before World War Two, the French ceded the *sanjak* (Ottoman administrative division) of Alexandretta, including the city of Antioch/Antakya and the port of Alexandretta/Iskenderun, to Turkey. The area, since called Hatay, had always been a socially and ethnically mixed area, but after the annexation many non-Turks migrated to Syria. These included Arabic-speaking Christians and Alawis who moved in large numbers to the cities of Aleppo and Lattakia. The migration sharpened their sense of Arabness. Socialist ideas also appealed to disadvantaged Alawites emerging from their centuries of marginalisation. The Ba'ath Party, founded by a Christian and a Sunni Muslim from Damascus, with its ideology of pan-Arabism and socialism, had a particular attraction for Alawis from the region of Lattakia.

For three years, from 1958 to 1961, Syria was a junior partner of the United Arab Republic. Although the rhetoric of the Republic was socialist and pan-Arab, Syrians were dominated by the senior partner under Gamal Abdul Nasser. The Ba'ath Party was actually banned during these years. Two years after the failed experiment of union with Egypt, the Ba'ath Party took over Syria in a coup. It has been in office ever since, though there have been important developments in the manner of its authority.

Throughout the 1960s the party's power was slowly narrowed, during which time Hafez al-Assad worked his way up, eliminating rivals to emerge at the top in November 1970. He was President for nearly thirty years, dying in June 2000. His personality has shaped modern Syria.

Hafez al-Assad was an Alawite from Qardaha, a village near Lattakia. He was a socialist and national student leader at secondary school. His vision for Syria was to emancipate the rural areas. Like many of comparable background, he escaped from poverty and joined the Air Force, passing through Homs Military Academy, and trained as a pilot. Hard working and persistent, he was impatient with others who had a different vision. During the union with Egypt he allied with others from the armed forces to form a 'Military Committee' of the Ba'ath Party that aimed at imposing their vision on the whole country. From the head of the Air Force he became Minister of Defence and, in that office, gave the order for withdrawal from the Golan Heights during the 1967 June War with Israel. The Ba'ath leader in those years was another socialist Alawite soldier, Salah al-Jadid. Hafez al-Assad pushed him aside in the autumn of 1970. Salah al-Jadid was seen as too ideological, and he spent the rest of his life in the old castle in Mezze, a political prison for senior politicians. He died there in August 1993.

Hafez al-Assad, though from an Alawi background, broadened the regime's base. Two of his closest allies who were loyal to him and to whom he was loyal were Sunnis from the rural north of the country. 'Abd al-Halim Khaddam was a student Ba'ath Party activist from the coastal town of Baniyas. He met Hafez al-Assad during the years of Assad's student activism. His first position was as Assad's Minister of Foreign Affairs and then as his Vice President. Mustafa Tlas was from Rastan, between Hama and Homs. He and Assad met in 1952 at the Homs Military Academy. He was made Minister of Defence in 1972 and held that post for the rest of Hafez al-Assad's life.

The Assad years were neither static nor monolithic. The president was popular in the first years when he reached out to the whole country. He built up a political system that drew ideas, willy nilly, from the Soviet Union. The Party made policy, Ministers executed it. There was a People's Assembly, carefully controlled and without any authority, and 'popular organisations' of the professions and the peasants. The Ba'ath Party was given precedence, though other allied parties – Communist,

Nasserist and socialist – were permitted to operate, albeit in a very circumscribed way. Assad was, every seven years, re-elected with 99 per cent of the vote or thereabouts. The background of the ministers and of the members of the People's Assembly, to a large extent, reflected the national breakdown of communities.

But aside from this formal system of governance there was an alternative informal system, based on the security apparatus. As a former conspirator, Assad excelled in maintaining the security of the regime. The *mukhabarat*, or secret police, was not the invention of the regime, however. The Ottomans had their spies. The French relied on intelligence services, and the pre-1970 regimes had their secret police. But by allowing Assad to take over power, these obviously failed. And so during the Assad years the security services were vastly expanded. There were half a dozen organisations, each headed by somebody who worked with total loyalty to Hafez al-Assad. The confrontation with Israel was the pretext and excuse for a State of Emergency which gave unrestricted and unaccountable authority to the security services. Public debate was stifled. The *mukhabarat* had files on everybody and its agents operated in every school, university, workplace, village and town quarter. By the 1990s it was reckoned that there were 100,000 full time members of the security forces. That means one for every 200 citizens. If we consider that over half the population is under twenty and that half is female, then that proportion comes down to one in fifty men. This also meant that every citizen may have had a relation, colleague, old school-fellow or neighbour who was a *mukhabarat* official at the operational level. However, the more senior a *mukhabarat* officer was, the more likely it was that he was an Alawite. Everybody was conscious of the power and unchallenged authority of the *mukhabarat*. Any political independence or potential activity against the regime was noted and perpetrators could expect to be called in for questioning, for rough interrogation, detention, and in many cases torture, disappearance and execution. Syria had one of the worst reputations for the abuse of human rights, though the abuses fluctuated over the decades.

Syrians learned to live with the *mukhabarat*. Discussion of politics was avoided. Rituals of overt support for the regime were observed, such as public applause at the name of the President. It was possible to lead a full life without politics, and, until 2011, the *mukhabarat* were interested in dissent rather than enforced assent. There were plenty of exceptions to this, and from time to time there were instances of arbitrary and capricious brutality. People were imprisoned without charge and without knowing why.

In the main cities non-Alawites were conscious of the concentration of power in the hands of this minority, many of whom came to occupy particular areas of those cities. Public policy was to ignore or overlook confessional differences, but an identifying accent or even body language was noted. The Assad years witnessed the emancipation of the Alawites. It is important however to recognise that there was no homogeneity amongst this community. There were clan and tribal differences. There were differences of class, between urban professionals and rural peasantry, between migrants from the *sanjak* of Alexandretta and the rest. Some religious leaders claimed a following, and it was revealing to discover who owed allegiance to particular religious leaders or their families. But Alawites in general, after centuries of oppression, became confident and assertive. They took to education, and the first generation of educated Alawites displayed a creativity beyond their numbers. For example, writers and intellectuals such as Hani al-Rahib, Sulaiman Ahmad, Sa'dallah Wannus, Mamduh Udwan and Bouthaina Shaaban achieved reputations that went beyond Syria and owed nothing to any privilege Alawites may have enjoyed. This generation of Alawites was politically active and it is reckoned that there was a disproportionate number of Alawites who were political prisoners.

Many Alawite intellectuals have moved into opposition since March 2011 – among them the writers Samar Yazbek and Rosa Yassin Hassan and the leftist Abdul Aziz al-Khayyar. Rasha Omran, an Alawite poet now living in exile, writes in this issue of *Critical Muslim* of her daughter's arrest by the state, and the unexpected responses of her Alawi friends and relatives to her family crisis. Omran was forced to confront the notion of 'identity', according to which 'My daughter and I constitute part of "Us", the power which protects its followers, a power we must follow simply because we share the sect of its leaders. According to this notion, citizenship enjoys the status of a fallen woman, belonging to the larger homeland means nothing at all, and security must stem from the narrowest sectarian allegiance'.

For some Sunni Muslims, Alawites were not Muslims. This troubled Hafez al-Assad. He showed a strange deference to formalities, and the constitution required the president to be a Muslim. Musa al-Sadr, the Shi'ite leader in Lebanon, issued a fatwa declaring that Alawites were indeed Muslims. Hafez al-Assad made a point of patronising Sunni Muslim clerics such as the Mufti, Ahmad Kaftaru, and Muhammad Sa'id al-Buti. In his later years he broke his habitual seclusion to come to the Umayyad Mosque for prayers for the Eid at the end of Ramadan. But for the older classes the simmering resentment of the Alawites and their dominance of the armed forces and the security services owed as much to class consciousness. The servants and peasants had taken over.

Under Hafez al-Assad there were four echelons of political power. The lowest level was that of ministers. They were like civil servants and could be appointed or dismissed at will. Apart from the ceremony of swearing in they may have had no personal contact with the president. But they had a budget and some patronage of their own and could build up their own fiefdoms, especially if they were in office for any length of time. And this was often the case. If people showed loyalty to the president, he returned that loyalty. He was also loath to change. For a well-established minister, his or her ministry became like a state within the state.

Above the ministers was the party. The Ba'ath Party had its branches throughout the country and the party secretary at any level had precedence over the formal official. The regional command of the party made policy and each ministry was shadowed by a member of that command. By the turn of the century there were a million party members. Membership and loyalty helped with employment prospects, although some Ministers were not members of the party. There were also hierarchies within the Party.

Above the party was the security apparatus which has been discussed. All management lines from the different security organisations led to the president himself.

It was around the person, the court as it were, that the top echelon of power could be found. Hafez al-Assad, a workaholic who toiled round the clock, took an interest in every appointment. Sometimes a minister had a direct link to the president or a member of his nuclear family. This link would endow the minister with greater authority, bypassing the party echelon and sometimes even the security apparatus. In his last years, the president rarely left his flat or his office. He was not generally visible and, apart from occasional overseas trips, did not get around the country much. It was reckoned that he did not go to Aleppo, the second city of the country, after the 1970s, and never went to Deir ez-Zor. Damascus and his home village of Qardaha were the limits of his travels within the country. Hafez al-Assad did not extend his circle and the 'court' was limited, although in the last years there was greater access to his sons. Other members of the family and his wife's family, the Makhloufs, were – to some extent – more accessible, extending the nature of 'court politics'. It was difficult to withstand the influence or requests of members of the families that were linked to the president.

Since the country's descent into the chaos of the last three years, it is easy to see the years of the two Assads as having always been rotten to the core. But this would be misleading and would also minimise the regime's achievements even though, under Hafez al-Assad, Syria steadily became a corrupt police state.

The forty Assad years had three remarkable and creditable achievements: socialism, stability and secularism.

The Ba'athist ideology was socialist. It aimed at a redistribution of power and resources, and the emancipation of the peasants. There was a redistribution programme, with a break-up of landed estates and nationalisations under successive governments, both before the union with Egypt and under the influence of Nasserist socialism. This led to a flight of businesses out of the country. However, under the Assads, and especially and consciously under Hafez al-Assad, Ba'athist ideology was inclusive. It was determined that every village should have access to fresh water, electricity, a health clinic and education. It could be argued that the quality of these services was often poor, but villages had not enjoyed these advantages before. Nor was this expansion of utilities and services unique to socialist Syria; the capitalist countries of the Arabian Peninsula had a similar positive record. Under the Assads it was theoretically possible for a poor child from a village, if he or she were bright enough, to receive free education from primary school to university. By the end of the century there were plenty of cases of people from poor rural backgrounds reaching the tops of the professions. Before the 1960s, power went to people, usually men, from the major cities. By the turn of the century, the elites included people from the rural west and the Euphrates Valley as well as from the major cities.

Before Hafez al-Assad assumed power in 1970, Syria was risibly notorious for its political instability. The country was subject to military coups – there were two in 1949 alone. It was impossible to plan ahead. It was unsettling, and inhibited people from investing in the country. The Assad regimes changed all that – up to 2011. The stability was gained at a price, as we have seen: the defences of stability restricted human rights in an appalling way. Hafez al-Assad was initially popular but faced challenges – from Islamists between 1978 and 1982 and from his brother in the 1980s. These challenges were faced with either brutal suppression, or with cunning personal diplomacy. The most traumatising of suppressions was the regime's massacre of somewhere between ten and forty thousand people in Hama in 1982 after the armed wing of the Muslim Brotherhood took over the city. By the 1990s all opposition had been crushed or exiled.

In her moving essay, Amal Hanano links the story of a woman who played dead under corpses in 1982 Hama to that of Anas, a man who had the same experience in Daraya in 2012. The woman used to write down what she had witnessed, then burn the pages, lest they were discovered. 'The process of writing and burning, remembering and repressing, speaking then falling silent,' Hanano writes, 'is the story of Syria under the rule of the Assad dynasty.' Of course, this all changed in 2011. Anas, and the new generation, no longer burn their stories:

When, in moments of weakness, you question, was our parents' silence better, smarter, stronger than our brothers' and sisters' chants? When you ask, were we really paying the price of silence, or did silence protect us then from the hell unleashed in Syria today? When doubt contaminates your beliefs, you go back to the woman in Hama who still burns her story. And you go back to Anas, who bravely tells his story over and over, so everyone is forced to listen and never forget.

But back in the eighties and nineties, for those who kept out of politics, the stability became a stasis, and people knew where they were. Syrian secularism drew on a liberal and open tradition epitomised by the two examples at the head of this essay. It was in the regime's interests to underplay confessionalism. Religious identity was manifest either by where you worshipped or whom you married. People were usually – but not always – aware of the religious identity of others. Aleppo and Damascus had their Muslim, Christian and Jewish quarters, but these were not sealed ghettos. In the countryside there were villages that were Muslim, Christian, Kurdish or Turcoman, but there were no villages or quarters exclusive to people of one confession. The wealthy urban Sunni elite was politically marginalised but prospered economically under the Assads. Hafez al-Assad fostered cordial relations with the largely Sunni business elite of Damascus, while the regime drew its support from poorer rural Muslims. We have seen how, from his twenties, Hafez al-Assad deliberately built his support nationally for ideological reasons. He presented himself as a Syrian Arab, not as an Alawite. When Islamism challenged Ba'athist rule in the years after 1978 he responded with savage repression. Yet many Syrians found this was a price worth paying when they saw what was happening in Lebanon in the 1980s or Algeria in the 1990s.

Hafez al-Assad died in June 2000. Like Gaddafi in Libya, Saddam Hussein in Iraq and Mubarak in Egypt – and one may add, like the rulers of all the countries in the Arabian peninsula – he wanted a son to succeed him as President. From the 1980s he was publicly addressed as Abu Basil, and his eldest son, Basil, was presented as heir. But Basil was killed driving at great speed on the way to the airport in January 1994. His younger brother Bashaar returned from ophthalmological training in London and assumed the role of heir apparent. Bashaar seemed more reflective, and was less flamboyant than his brother. He received military training and rapid promotion, travelled around the country and quickly became more visible and approachable than his father.

After the father died, a constitutional process – albeit with expeditious amendment – was launched to appoint a successor. Bashaar was duly elected as Secretary General of the Ba'ath Party and as president. He seemed a breath of fresh air. He was a computer buff and seemed to be aware of the outside world in a way his father never was. The first months of his presidency were full of hope. He wandered around the city of Damascus with minimum security. He married a dashing London Syrian girl (whose father was a doctor in London but whose family were Sunni merchants from Homs). They ate out in public. He seemed to encourage open debate, a freer press. Political prisoners were released and Damascus saw political forums debate previously taboo issues. Afra Jalabi, who contributes an essay to this issue, was a signatory to the Damascus Declaration, formed in 2005 as an umbrella group to create an indigenous political alliance to push for gradual change.

But the Damascus spring was followed by a Damascus winter. Press restrictions were reinstated. Dissidents were rearrested. Others went into exile. As for Afra Jalabi and her Damascus Declaration colleagues, 'most of the initial 200 signatories inside Syria were imprisoned, and those of us in the diaspora who signed it found ourselves on Syrian security lists, unable to visit the country again'. Jalabis describes her 'first visit in years' to the 'liberated' territories of the north, which are certainly not liberated from the threat of air strikes.

Bashaar constantly promised reforms but hinted that political reforms should only follow after economic reforms. He had been under pressure, especially from the European Union, to liberalise the economy, and as a result, in the early years of the century state enterprises were denationalised, private banks were founded, and the public sector monopoly of higher education ended. As in the former Soviet Union, this resulted in greater freedom for a few, but an increased disparity in wealth. The beneficiaries were all people close to the regime. Sons of favoured generals and of others near the court of the President – *awlad al-sulta*, 'sons of those in power', they were called – made massive fortunes. Smart restaurants charging European prices flourished. To the west of Damascus, villas with swimming pools were built behind security walls. For a while there was even a casino.

But there were other developments over which Bashaar had no control. Most Syrians have connections outside the country: migrants who have settled in Europe, the United States or South America; men and women who have studied abroad; temporary, but long term, residents in the Gulf states; the middle classes who have taken holidays in Europe, or closer to home in Cyprus or Turkey; a working class who have worked for US$20 a day in Lebanon. Since the 1960s many men, especially of the articulate middle class, have married foreign wives. Their children, who could be called *awlad al-ʿālam* (children of the world), were bicultural, unquestionably Syrian, but with an awareness of international standards (if not practices) of liberty and openness. They had grown up with the information revolution that has destroyed the self-deluding propaganda of totalitarian regimes. They could see how Bashaar was failing to meet the expectations of his first few years. The regime's legitimacy crumbled.

The Arab Spring was delayed in its arrival in Syria. In January 2011 Bashaar al-Assad gave an interview to *The Wall Street Journal* in which he said that Syria was stable, unlike the surrounding Arab states, because the regime was close to the beliefs of the people. Two months later the southern city of Dara'a was in revolt and by March there were demonstrations in the capital.

Drought in the years before 2011 had led to a migration from rural areas to the outer suburbs of the big cities. Dara'a, in the centre of an agricultural region, was badly affected, and schoolboys scribbled 'The people want the downfall of the regime' on walls. There was an immediate cruel and insensitive response. In the spring the first demonstrations took place in the major cities. At first the opposition was not directly challenging the regime. Specific demands were made, echoing the demands of the Damascus Spring ten years earlier. Demonstrators waved yellow cards, like a football referee giving a player a warning rather than sending him off. Early demonstrations were particularly strong in the neglected rural areas – ironically just those areas from which the Ba'athist regime had originally derived their strongest support. The demonstrations in Damascus led to state-organised counter-demonstrations in support of the regime. It was observed that the pro-Bashaar demonstrators were smartly dressed, the new prosperous beneficiaries of neo-liberal economic policies (although many were civil servants and schoolchildren bussed in).

Demonstrations were brutally suppressed, suspects were rounded up and tortured. By late 2011 the infrastructure of the country was imploding. Syria broke down into the hell that we have been witnessing ever since.

Why has this happened? Although the President and his court are at the apex of the echelons of power in the country, there have always been multiple power structures. Hafez al-Assad was able to manage these, but Bashaar lacks the cunning of his father. There is another big difference between father and son. The father was a young idealist. He had a vision of a socialist Syria – breaking up the traditional urban powers, and emancipating the peasants. In this he succeeded, albeit at a high cost. He was ready to reward those loyal to him and to mercilessly crush any who got in his way. By contrast, Bashaar was born to privilege. Such vision as he had has been hesitant and inarticulate. But he has been decisive in defending the privileges of his court and of those who are loyal to him, principally the security services and the armed gangs, the *shabiha*, who have raided, beaten up, tortured and killed on behalf of the regime. Steadily over his first decade of power, the popular support he initially enjoyed was squandered. During the course of 2011 the regime lost control of large swathes of the country. The opposition was fragmented and there seemed to be an increase in the perpetration of atrocities. Insecure borders have allowed adventurers, mercenaries and fanatics to add to the misery of ordinary Syrians. The parts the government did control, or where they were able to re-establish control, faced confident and unrestrained security forces. Apart from the concerted support from Russia and Iran, it has been suggested that the resilience of the regime is because of the extensive work of the *mukhabarat* spying on the population over the previous forty years, as well as the establishment of a network of air bases throughout the country. It was as if the regime had always been preparing for this crisis.

It is impertinent for a non-Syrian to propose a solution. The civil war has acquired its own momentum. But there has been nothing inevitable about the conflict, which is a repudiation of the habits and traditions in Syria that have prevailed over centuries if not millennia. It is a Syrian conflict and it is for Syrians to find their way out, with the support, help and encouragement of their friends.

The end of all this is obscure, and the present reality a cause of controversy. In the pages to come, Ella Wind finds that 'a strong tension exists between outside and inside perspectives, between journalistic storylines and anecdotal accounts'. Her essay undermines the stereotypes and false assumptions of media representations by describing two men she knew in Syria in 2011, film-maker Bassel Shahadeh, killed by regime bombs, and Father Paolo Dall'Oglio, a prominent Jesuit priest first exiled by the regime then abducted by the Islamic State of Iraq and Syria. In these pages too, Louis Proyect castigates the failure of Islamophobic left-liberal intellectuals to respond intelligently to the crisis, taking particular aim at the *New Yorker* and *London Review of Books*.

In these last years, Syrian culture has been revolutionised, for good and for ill. Maysaloon's essay for this issue depicts the rise of Syrian drama serials in recent decades, and their hidden complicity with regime priorities. Dan Gorman and Yasmin Fedda, on the other hand, explore the history of subversive documentary production. Frederic Gijsel offers a vision of a raucous Damascene poetry club in the final moments before revolution, and Itab Azzam provides an account of how she persuaded refugee women to participate in a production of Euripides' *Trojan Women*. Robin Yassin-Kassab considers the enormous cultural rupture caused by the revolution, the explosion of 'low-brow' revolutionary art, of revolutionary newspapers and radio stations, and of experiments in local self-organisation.

What else lies within these covers? There is prose from Zakaria Tamer, master of the Arabic very short story, and poetry from the accomplished Kurdish-Syrian poet Golan Haji, and still much more. For now, the last word must go to Amal Hanano, who sums up the immediacy of today's Syrian turmoil: 'We awakened not only to fight the oppression and brutality that had defined us. We awakened to discover who we were.'

REVOLUTIONARY CULTURE

Robin Yassin-Kassab

In 'Assad's Syria', as the slogans at the borders and in the streets called it, schools taught by rote and intimidation. The universities were ideologically policed. Trade unions were controlled by the state and the Ba'ath Party (these two inextricably intertwined). Beyond the Ba'ath's various paramilitary organisations and the closely monitored mosques and churches, there was no civil society under Hafez al-Assad. Later, the regime's 'quasi'-NGOs, run by Bashaar al-Assad's wife Asma or other members of the ruling family, provided only a parody of civil society which aimed, in the words of dissident Ammar Abdulhamid, 'to crowd out the real independent organisations'. State TV, radio and newspapers churned out pictures of the Leader and endless footage of grim-faced citizens shaking weak fists in 'spontaneous expressions of love and loyalty'. Hafez al-Assad went in for totalitarian culture of the North Korean variety – for example, choreographed spectacles in sports stadiums which effaced hundreds of people's identities to spell out slogans praising the president. Grim metal statues of Assad stared down over university campuses and shopping streets. Stepped altars to the dictator's image lined the inter-city highways. Like the Prophet Muhammad, the president was titled al-Ameen, as-Sadeeq (the Truthful, the Trustworthy). Syrians joked in muted tones about the oft-portrayed Holy Trinity of father (Hafez), son (Bashaar), and holy ghost (the eldest son Basil, known as 'the role model', killed while speeding on the airport road). In school *Qowmiya* (nationalism) classes, Qur'anic quotations ('God, may He be glorified and exalted, said…') were interspersed with the president's words ('President Leader Hafez al-Assad, the Struggling Comrade, said…'). After his death, Hafez was declared 'the Eternal Leader'.

Most Syrians, of course, did not adopt the religion of Assadism, though its icons decorated their streets, shops and cars. Syria scholar Lisa Wedeen's book *Ambiguities of Domination* asks why the regime invested so much money and effort in a propaganda structure which was so obviously ineffective, and finds that the intention was not to convince the public but to undermine the public space, to destroy the integrity of those forced into hypocrisy, and to debase the meaning of language itself. Syrians behaved 'as if' they loved the regime, even praising the president in front of their children out of fear the children might repeat the wrong thing in public. A culture of hypocrisy and opportunism spread, and nobody expected honesty. In this way, and by brute demonstrations of power (most notably the 1982 Hama massacre), Assad Senior achieved his kingdom of silence.

When Bashaar inherited the state at the turn of the century, neo-liberal economic reforms combined with nepotism to destroy the old quasi-socialist safety net for the rural and suburban proletariat and the lower middle class. Crony capitalism became part of the culture (making Bashaar's cousin Rami Makhlouf by far the richest man in the country), increasing poverty and social division, and undercutting the old contract whereby (some) previously marginalised classes and regions were brought closer to the economic centre. This ill-named *infitah* or 'opening' meant that coffee at (Saudi prince) Waleed bin Talal's Four Seasons (built on demolished Ottoman town houses) cost half a week's working-class wage. At the same time, the Old City of Damascus was revived by boutique hotels, fine restaurants, bars and art galleries. The old Damascus families couldn't afford the property prices, and moved to the suburbs, the fringes of which were increasingly inhabited by the poor unemployed or underpaid, many of them climate-change refugees from the ignored and desertifying east.

For about six months after Bashaar's ascension it looked as if a gradual 'Damascus Spring' would breathe new life into the stagnant political and cultural spheres. A number of long-term political prisoners were released. Some of the ubiquitous pro-regime graffiti was painted over. There were notably fewer posters of the president on the walls. Cartoonist Ali Farzat's *al-Domari* (*The Lamplighter*), with its weekly diet of satire and investigative journalism, was the most provocative of the newly licensed publications. Political discussion groups were set up in private homes, and dissenting intellectuals issued declarations calling for greater political freedom. But almost immediately the spring faded back to winter. Those intellectuals who had been encouraged to engage in constructive criticism were arrested and imprisoned on spurious charges. Private but regime-affiliated media (usually owned by the president's relatives and friends) aimed to smother, and provide a simulacrum of, a genuine free press. *Al-Domari* was closed.

Yet state censorship was inevitably less efficacious than in earlier decades. Access to al-Jazeera and other satellite channels was widespread, and internet use spread steadily. Though the internet was carefully monitored, young Syrians soon became experts in cheating the authorities via proxy servers. The new technology meant that despite the best efforts of the supposedly Arabist regime, Syrians in the years before the revolution had never been in closer touch with the Arabs in their various countries, especially the young and politically restless.

And so it was in the remaining fields of culture, a process of push and pull between state repression and a society hungering for new horizons. The people resisted passively with dark humour and a gruff irony, and made their own evening entertainments with oud and song. The more elitist and politically neutral visual arts flourished in the Bashaar years, as did historical and fantasy television drama. More provocative arts lived either underground or on the edges of the visible. Books, either permitted or smuggled from elsewhere, were discussed in private conversations. Poetry remained a popular and often subversive commentary on social realities and – because orality and memorisation are still important elements of Syrian culture – poems were as difficult to censor as the internet.

Two of the late-twentieth-century greats were Nizar Qabbani and Muhammad al-Maghout. The former spent much of the Ba'athist period in exile, in Lebanon and London, but his anti-traditional love poems and his devastating political poetry (against social backwardness and dictatorship, and on nationalist themes) were equally well-known in Syria and throughout the Arab world. Al-Maghout's poetry was far less romantic and perhaps more in keeping with the times than Qabbani's (his narrative personas are more likely to be leering lechers than self-annihilating lovers), and his prose satires, though they named no names, were savage. Nevertheless, Maghout was tolerated and perhaps even grudgingly admired by Hafez al-Assad.

Playwright Sa'adullah Wannous was another who somehow got away with it. His proto-revolutionary *The Elephant, O Lord of Ages* was even performed (in both Arabic and English – translated by Peter Clark, who writes the introduction to this issue) in central Damascus. Other favourites who danced on the boundaries include comedians Yasser al-Azmeh, whose 'Maraya' dared to poke fun at the secret police, and Durayd Lahham, who starred in biting satirical films (scripted by Muhammad al-Maghout) on the failures of Arab nationalism, perhaps the best of which is *al-Hudood* (The Borders). By approving such work, the regime gave the impression that it was the other regimes that were guilty of corruption and self-interest, and that were it not for them it would have solved pan-Arab challenges.

Two illuminating Syrian novels of late-twentieth-century dictatorship, both available in English (and both banned but clandestinely available in Syria), are screenwriter and novelist Nihad Sirees's *The Silence and the Roar*, a tragi-comic dystopia to match Orwell or Huxley, and Khaled Khalifa's masterful *In Praise of Hatred*, which dramatises rival ideologies in 1980s Aleppo, torn between the Muslim Brothers and the regime.

The totalitarian period also produced notable prison literature, most recently *The Shell* (not yet published in English) by Mustafa Khalifa, who was imprisoned without charge or trial between 1982 and 1994. For so many intellectuals and writers, prison (and the inevitable mistreatment that goes with prison) was a formative experience. Others include the political thinker Yassin al-Haj Saleh and the poet Faraj Bayrakdar.

Precisely because of the savage degree of repression, it seemed to many (including me) that the Arab revolution which erupted in Tunisia in the last days of 2010 wouldn't reach as far as Syria. The first Facebook calls for protest mobilised almost nobody. Traumatic memories of Hama, fear of sectarian breakdown, the near complete absence of political networks and civil movements, the presumed nationalism of the regime (its 'resistance' image still impressed some at home) – these factors combined seemed to ensure the regime's stability. When Mubarak fell, Syrian TV showed al-Jazeera's live feed of the celebrations in Tahrir Square. This was a message to the people that the regime had nothing to fear, that its self-confidence and sense of legitimacy were unshaken.

On 17 February 2011, police beat up the son of a merchant in the Hareeqa area of central Damascus. (*Hareeqa* means 'Fire', and is so named because it was burnt by French bombs during the 1925–1927 anti-colonial uprising.) Such brutality would usually pass with only a little muttering; this time the merchants and labourers of the neighbourhood apprehended the guilty policemen, then gathered in their hundreds and chanted 'The Syrian People Won't be Humiliated'. The regime sent the Interior Minister to the scene. He asked the crowd if this was a demonstration. No, they responded; but it clearly was – not only a protest against repression, but a sign of an entirely new mood.

Next, the torture of the boys in Dara'a who had scrawled revolutionary slogans on the walls. Then the murder of the boys' protesting relatives. Then an expanding circle of protests, murders, and larger protests, spreading over the entire country, involving every class, ethnicity and sect.

Bashaar was a popular figure until his first, belated speech of the crisis. People expected an apology and an announcement of serious reform; instead they heard giggles and wild conspiracy theories. And every day the killings, beatings and humiliations accumulated. When thirteen-year-old Hamza al-Khateeb's horribly tortured corpse was returned to his parents, Syrians responded with a visceral outrage that startled even themselves. One face on the screen defined the moment: 'I am not an animal!' proclaimed this man with wide-open eyes, as if it was a new discovery.

Syrians stopped acting 'as if', and shocked themselves in the process. Participants often describe their first protest as an almost mystical experience of liberation through honest self-expression, of breaching the limits imposed by fear, and of finding true solidarity with the community. Those who entered the revolution had a sense of being reborn as citizens rather than as subjects, as agents of Syrian destiny rather than mere extras in the Assad epic.

Revolutionary Syrians discovered the country anew. At protests they learnt the Kurdish word for freedom (*azadi*) and recited the names of towns and villages of which they'd never previously heard, but which were suddenly centres of the revolutionary culture: Kafranbel, Amouda, Da'el, al-Bayda, and so on.

Regime supporters, meanwhile, emphasised a Syrian identity which excluded the majority of Syrians. These barbarians, they explained, were protesting in Hama because the city had always been a centre of Islamist reaction; in Dara'a and Deir ez-Zor the people were shoeless Beduin; in

Idlib they were ignorant peasants; in the Damascus suburbs they were poverty-stricken fanatics; and the Homsis (the butt of a million Syrian jokes) had always been stupid.

Even as the death count rose, many figures of the established official culture declared loyalty to the regime and its narrative of foreign infiltration. These included the 'nationalist' comedian Durayd Lahham and pop star George Wassouf, seen on video singing to, and kissing the hand of, Bashaar's cousin Rami Makhlouf. Others, such as the Paris-based modernist poet Adonis, who for decades had been a critic of dictatorship and cultural stagnation but now strangely referred to Bashaar as 'the elected president', appeared more scared of Islamism, perhaps of Islam, than of the regime's terror and its sectarian propaganda (this was long before Salafist groups became prominent in the armed opposition). But many more took pro-revolutionary positions. Some examples: actress Mai Skaf was arrested for protesting; cartoonist Ali Farzat had his hands broken by regime thugs for caricaturing Bashaar; novelists Khaled Khalifa, Samar Yazbek and Fadi Azzam wrote for the revolution and against the repression, as did poets Golan Hajji and Rasha Omran; and musician Sameeh Shuqair wrote and sang *Ya Haif* ('For shame, brother, for shame! Shooting the defenceless – for shame! How can you arrest young children? You are a son of this country but you kill its children. You turn your back to the enemy but you assault us with a sword.') It is significant that several figures on this very limited list are from minority communities, including Assad's own Alawi community. Their presence in the revolution therefore contradicted the regime's sectarian narrative.

But the real cultural change was the explosion of 'low-brow' art and commentary in the revolution, from the increasingly creative protest chants through street poetry and dancing to revolutionary songs.

In Da'el, for instance, the romantic song *Ya Sari Sar al-Lail* was transformed into an anti-regime march. In Hama, Ibrahim Qashoush led the crowd in *Irhal, ya Bashaar!* (Leave, Bashaar!), a song which rapidly became an anthem of the revolution. (The regime's artistic response was to rip out Qashoush's vocal chords before throwing his corpse in the Orontes.) On the internet, Syria's hip hop and metal groups added their noise. A host of short video projects expressed revolutionary hopes and criticism, the 'Top Goon' puppet shows being one of the most accomplished. Alongside the engaged art of established painters abroad like Ibrahim Jalal, younger artists like Tammam Azzam and Wissam al-Jazairy designed shocking and inspiring internet images. The 'Stamps of the Syrian Revolution' project sought to symbolically reclaim sovereignty and national identity from the tyrannous state by defining its own set of national heroes, including figures of the anti-colonial struggle alongside contemporary activists, intellectuals, artists and martyrs. Syrians, supposedly cut off by tyranny from the flow of global culture, proved themselves adept students of international media and its popular culture references. Kafranbel, for instance, a small town in Idlib province, became nationally and then internationally known for the witty and media-savvy slogans and cartoons (in Arabic and English) displayed at the Friday demonstration.

Many foreign commentators read the uprising through their habitual journalistic or Area Studies prisms, ones often tinged with Orientalism. They saw the sectarian breakdown as fated and inevitable even before the regime and its allies managed to engineer it, and therefore they missed one of the most remarkable features of the revolution – the miracle of a non-sectarian freedom movement in a country which, despite the cheery official talk of a happy mosaic, was certainly riven beneath the surface by sectarian, ethnic and class cleavages (the Alawi-dominated regime, like the French before, had sustained these divisions in order to rule). One of the most prominent early protest chants was *Wahed, Wahed, Wahed, ash-Sha'ab as-Suri Wahed* (One, One, One, the Syrian People are One); in besieged Sunni areas of Homs, the Alawi actress Fadwa Suleiman led the chant *La Ikhwan Wala Salafiya: Kulna Bidna al-Hurriyyeh* (No Muslim Brotherhood and No Salafism: We All Want Freedom). Nabd (Pulse), formed in 2011, is an organisation specifically targeting the threat of sectarianism. It organises protests which include people of all backgrounds, particularly in secular strongholds and mixed communities such as Homs, Yabroud, Selemiyyeh and Zabadani; its Alawi and Ismaili members smuggle aid and supplies into (largely Sunni) areas under siege; and it reaches out to pro-regime communities.

What this anti-sectarian activism demonstrated was not so much an absence of sectarian identification amongst the younger generation as a strikingly intelligent analysis of the challenge ahead. Their political elites abroad failed them, but Syrians on the ground had learnt the lessons of the clash between Islamists and the regime in the 1980s, and of the sectarian civil wars in Lebanon and Iraq. They knew the regime would play on sect to retain power; they knew the fear of sectarian breakdown would keep many on the sidelines of the revolution. And it's notable that this movement was by no means restricted to islands of bourgeois cosmopolitanism in Damascus and Aleppo – all-Sunni farming communities and the poor inner cities understood and promoted the unity imperative as much as anyone else.

Despite the provocations, the new discourse of shared dignity in citizenship remained dominant for the first year and a half, and still survives today. It is perhaps the revolution's greatest victory; the fact that after 2012 it was overshadowed by an increasingly virulent identity politics is perhaps the greatest tragedy brought about by the counter-revolution. The regime engineered this, first by a propaganda effort, then by sending irregular *shabeeha* militias (in the Homs, Hama and Lattakia areas, these were almost entirely manned by Alawis) into Sunni areas to slaughter, rape, torture and burn. And when Iran and its client militias (including Lebanon's Hizbullah, once wildly popular amongst Syrians) reorganised Assad's failing front-line, the ethnically cleansed and the dispossessed gradually came to see themselves as victims of an Alawi-Shia front. Now this too is part of the culture, alongside the discourse of common citizenship: a mutual demonisation enacted through video clips, sectarian anthems, and physical assaults on the other side's religious heritage.

One very positive feature of revolutionary Syria is the plethora of exercises in self-government that emerged in response to the repression and the collapse of state services. Hundreds of local councils throughout the country – many chosen in free elections, the first in Syria in over four decades – document deaths and arrests, organise protests and civil disobedience campaigns, and provide aid and humanitarian supplies to areas under regime siege. In liberated areas, the councils organise health, education, sanitation, and power as best they can under desperate conditions. Umbrella groups which link up the councils on regional and national levels include the Local Coordination Committees (LCCs), the National Action Committees (NACs), the Federation of the Coordination Committees of the Syrian Revolution (FCCs), and the Syrian Revolution

General Commission (SRGC). This is the grassroots framework of Syria's most hopeful future, and if anti-aircraft defences ever protect these territories from Assad's scorched-earth-from-the-air policy, the base would have opportunity to grow, the refugees could return home, an alternative could be proven. But the bombs continue to fall...

In parts of the country, *shari'a* courts sprang up where the civil courts collapsed, and these varied greatly. In some areas they were imposed by one brand or other of Islamist militia, and focused on restricting individual freedoms, particularly those of women, and suppressing political dissent; in other areas they were worthwhile grassroots community initiatives to redress grievances and ensure basic security after the collapse of the state.

And Syrians took control of their media. They uploaded phonescreen videos to YouTube, hundreds of thousands of them, making the Syrian revolution and the various counter-revolutions the most documented of any events in history. Beyond Syria, meanwhile, a new media subset emerged: bloggers and analysts – the weapons expert Elliot Higgins is perhaps the most influential – who cross-reference and examine the YouTube raw material to build a picture of the war, the forces and arms in play. If the world is confused as to what is happening in Syria, no blame can be assigned to the revolutionary people. Thousands of citizen journalists and photographers risk their lives to get the story out; very many have died.

In this country, where ten years ago the existence of one satirical paper (*al-Domari*) seemed an enormous leap forward, today there are at least fifty-nine independent newspapers and magazines, including the collectively-managed *Oxygen*, from Zabadani, and *Aneb Baladi* (Local Grapes), established by women in the besieged, starved and bombarded suburb of Darraya, near Damascus.

The revolution has brought dramatic change to the culture where it's most immediately significant, in people's personal lives. Conservative women have come out of seclusion to do social work; others have defied their fathers to put on the hijab in solidarity with their neighbours, or to take the hijab off, or even to take up arms and fight. Soldiers have disobeyed their officers; men who once acted only for profit are now motivated by principle. Syrians are questioning authority on every level – that of the regime and of those attempting to replace the regime, of

Islamists and secularists, of traditional leaders and of the new ones who fail. Civil society is protesting against the regime, against the PYD (Democratic Union Party, the organisation currently dominating Syrian Kurdistan), against the corruption or intolerance of local Free Army militias, and against the mainly foreign-manned al-Qaeda offshoot the Islamic State of Iraq and Syria (ISIS).

The culture of resistance is based on a culture of criticism. Short of large-scale genocide or a permanent ethnic cleansing (neither possibility can be discounted), this cultural vivacity can't be returned to the box. The revolution has changed Syrian social dynamics irrevocably.

Yet so many have been killed, detained, or exiled. So many have been raped or otherwise humiliated. What was once a 'middle-income' country is an economic wasteland. A generation of children enters the twenty-first century without schooling. For that matter, without vaccination, and with polio, typhoid, tuberculosis. A generation of orphans, of children who have known terror, who have seen the roof cave in, their uncle stabbed to death, their father in abject panic. What will this bring?

For most Syrians today, survival comes first and last. Their culture is one of war, displacement, rupture, trauma. Over the past three years some have stooped to astounding depths of savagery; others have engaged with the turmoil in unexpectedly inspiring and beautiful ways. No-one can say which impulse, or what combination of impulses, will win the future. This uncertainty too is revolution.

THE REVOLUTION'S ARMED ISLAMISTS

Sam Charles Hamad

For many observers in the West, the Syrian revolution has been defined by the threat of imperialism; that is, by the notion that the Western imperialist powers would co-opt the popular struggle against the Assad regime for their own ends. While this thinking has proved erroneous, imperialism has indeed been a devil on the back of the Syrian revolution. But not in the way that one might immediately imagine. At this moment in the revolution, when the Assad regime has managed (by way of massive military aid from Russia and direct intervention from both the Islamic Republic of Iran and their theocratic proxies in Hizbullah) to hammer out a bloody stalemate with the fractured, isolated, increasingly sectarian and materially emaciated armed rebel factions, it is ludicrous to imagine that the main problem facing the revolution is an excess of support from the West. Yet this has been the charge from certain so-called 'anti-imperialist' quarters.

When one thinks of imperialism in the modern era, one thinks of the interventions in Iraq and Afghanistan, and one assumes straightaway that imperialism's prime danger is its incessant and malign interference. One does not immediately consider imperialism's other side, namely its cold and amoral indifference to the worst kinds of human suffering, and to those struggling against the very well-supported causes of such suffering. Indeed, the Syrian revolution and the lack of material support for those forces leading it should provide the final nail in the coffin of the notion of 'humanitarian intervention', if the Iraq war had not already left this concept dead and buried. Sadly, the leadership of the moderate civil and military opposition forces in Syria have yet to realise this fact, and have therefore organised on the basis of what has been a series of red herrings (forget 'red lines') of supposed Western support.

During the night of 6 December 2013, at the Bab al-Hawa crossing on the north-western border with Turkey, a major shift occurred in the balance of forces of the armed revolutionary formations. Several warehouses belonging to the Free Syrian Army (FSA), which up until this point had been the main (and most moderate) force among the armed opposition to Assad, were seized by the newly formed Islamic Front (IF), a coalition of hard-line Islamist anti-Assad groups. For many Western observers, this action represented the new dominance of what are invariably lumped together as the opposition's 'Islamists'. *The Independent's* Middle East correspondent Patrick Cockburn saw it as a failure of 'Western foreign policy', even going so far as to compare the situation to the Western arming of Afghan *mujahideen* against Soviet occupation forces in the 1980s.

Many Western observers believe that the West's 'interference' has led to 'jihadis' becoming the dominant force in the revolution. However, the opposite is true. The incident at Bab al-Hawa was indicative of the major problem faced by the moderate opposition forces — a lack of material support leading to their marginalisation and the increasing dominance of Islamists. In order to fully understand this without resorting to crude Afghan analogies, or without acceding to the logic of the Assad regime that the entire opposition is 'al-Qaeda' or 'jihadis', it is important to separate out the major factions and to explore their aims and ideological motivations, how they relate to each other and to the civil opposition in exile that purports to lead the revolution, and to the Western powers and allies in the Gulf Cooperation Council.

It should be remembered that it was the Assad regime that made armed opposition necessary and inevitable. The Syrian revolution started out, like the uprisings in Tunisia and Egypt, with mass protests characterised by non-violent civil disobedience. Unlike the regimes of Ben Ali and Mubarak, the Assad regime responded to the protests with live ammunition and mass murder. With orders coming from the very top to shoot unarmed protesters, some officers in the Syrian Arab Army (SAA) refused to comply and defected to the revolutionaries; thus the Free Syrian Army (FSA) was born and the revolutionary war erupted.

Despite the fact that the core of the FSA is comprised of former SAA soldiers and officers, the majority of its forces are revolutionary civilian volunteers. So the FSA is very much an ad hoc fighting force – its 'brigades' are only loosely connected and are structurally diverse and it relies on resources that are close to hand, such as weaponry and equipment that came with the original defections and whatever can be captured on the battlefield. Contrary to the thoroughly misleading mantra repeated so widely in the Western media of the FSA being 'Western backed', which implies a certain level of material support, the reality is that the FSA has received only small, intermittent shipments of mostly light weaponry sourced from Gulf states.

While it's easy to be pessimistic about the course of the revolutionary war and the fate of the FSA as an ideologically moderate fighting force capable of forming a security apparatus in a post-Ba'athist Syria, the armed struggle has nevertheless ensured that vast swathes of Syria remain out of the control of the Assad regime. Yet no force has been capable of penetrating the heart of the regime and snuffing out its lifelines. This has led to a bloody stalemate in which the regime employs its air force and sophisticated artillery capabilities to constantly bombard the rebel-held territories – it is this aspect of Assad's counter-insurgency that has not only led to massive civilian casualties and the displacement of civilian populations, but has also exacerbated the isolation and division of the Free Army brigades around the country and the almost impossible task of imposing any sort of leadership on them. The civilian leaders, such as the Syrian National Coalition (SNC) and its counterpart set up to lead the Free Army, the Supreme Military Council (SMC), are forced to conduct their business in exile in Turkey, and are thus perceived as out of touch with the realities of the revolution on the ground.

In contrast to Libya, where not only was a NATO no-fly zone set up, allowing Benghazi to become the social, political and military hub of the revolution against Gaddafi, but where revolutionaries were also provided with sophisticated anti-aircraft weaponry such as MANPADS, the Syrian revolutionaries have been left to their fate under Assad's Russian war planes, leading to an ever-widening gulf between the political and armed wings of the revolution. In this environment, it doesn't take long for dissent to set in.

With no possibility of establishing a base within Syria, the exiled opposition have been at the mercy of foreign governments. Thus far, the exiled opposition's plan has been that if foreign powers would provide aid, they would distribute it and thereby win the authority to organise the revolutionary ranks from above. This would have certainly been a sound strategy had it not been for the fact that foreign powers, specifically the United States, have not been forthcoming with aid, but have in fact actively blocked other powers, such as Saudi Arabia, Qatar and the new revolutionary government in Libya, from supplying the rebel forces with the heavy weaponry needed to match the regime and take on its air force. Moreover, the Coalition's reliance on foreign powers has worsened its ideological divisions. The two largest backers of the opposition, Qatar and Saudi Arabia, have attempted to further their own interests by backing one faction over another, which has led to almost constant infighting.

This brings us back to that December night in 2013 when the Islamic Front took over FSA facilities at Bab al-Hawa. The longstanding detractors of the Syrian revolution felt themselves vindicated by the fact that 'Islamism' had become so visibly dominant on the ground. Again, the growing dominance of the Islamist groups in the armed struggle is a direct result of the lack of support for the moderate opposition groups and the failed strategy of the exiled opposition in constantly chasing foreign support that was never going to materialise. The intensity and complexity of the grass roots struggle on the ground demanded a level of organisational and structural support that the exiled opposition has so far been unable to provide. The Islamic Front, on the other hand, has employed almost the exact opposite strategy in terms of organising, and it has reaped the rewards.

On 22 November 2013, seven hard-line Islamist brigades announced they were merging into one large fighting force to be known as the Islamic Front. Estimates put its numbers at somewhere between 40,000 and 70,000 men. Accompanying this announcement, a charter laid out the IF's ideology and aims in very general terms. For many Syrians on the ground and abroad, and for many non-Syrian observers and supporters of the revolution, the most worrying aspects of the IF are its Salafi ideology, the sectarian rhetoric of its leaders, and its rejection of secular democracy. In the midst of a revolutionary war against a tyranny rooted in sectarianism, these factors led many to conclude that the IF was in fact similar to such counter-revolutionary jihadist *takfiri* (Muslims who accuse other Muslims of being apostates) formations as the Islamic State of Iraq and al-Sham (ISIS). The fact of the IF's seizure of FSA facilities at Bab al-Hawa did nothing to assuage these fears, although the situation was amicably resolved, with both the IF and the FSA putting it down to a mere misunderstanding, as opposed to the beginning of a new intra-rebel war.

If the Arab revolutions have taught us anything, it is that 'Islamism' is a deeply inadequate blanket term laced with post-9/11 prejudices and fears. According to the standard definition, the term implies a spectrum covering ideologically disparate groups, from moderate and democratic forces such as the Egyptian Muslim Brotherhood to the *takfiri* ISIS and other groups associated with al-Qaeda. In this context, while it is true that the Islamic Front rejects democracy and secularism in favour of an Islamic state, it also makes it very clear that, unlike ISIS, it does not wish to impose its ideology on the people of Syria. Its charter does not go into detail about its vision of a future Islamic state, but rather places emphasis on the fact that its primary aim is to overthrow Assad.

In the context of its rise – a bloody war against a much better armed regime, and a faltering secular leadership that put itself at the mercy of imperialist powers which failed to deliver – IF ideology is less important than the fact that it has a greater ability than its moderate counterparts to provide its cadres with weaponry and equipment. Indeed, as Aaron Lund, writing for the Carnegie Endowment for Global Peace, points out, several moderate Free Army brigades have defected to the IF, adopting Islamist rhetoric in order to gain access to weaponry and resources that the leadership of the FSA has been unable to provide.

The IF has been able to successfully place itself between the forces on the ground allied to the exiled opposition and reliant on Western and Gulf aid on the one hand, and those forces that are hostile to the West, such as Jabhat al-Nusra (JaN), a branch of al-Qaeda. There is speculation that the IF is funded by Saudi Arabia, and its military leader, Zahran Alloush, is thought to be close to the Saudi regime, but there have also been rumours that it is connected to Qatar. Whatever the reality of these claims, the fact is that while its capabilities are still relatively weak and it remains susceptible to defections and internal strife, it has managed not just to effectively function outside of the fold of the official opposition, but to flourish by doing so.

During the opposition's Lattakia offensive in August 2013, around 190 Alawi civilians were murdered by extremist Islamists in what remains, at the time of writing, the only large-scale sectarian slaughter perpetrated by anti-Assad forces (a string of sectarian massacres have been committed by Assad's *shabeeha* militias). Human Rights Watch accused the two al-Qaeda-associated groups ISIS and JaN of involvement, as well as the IF's Ahrar ash-Sham group. Ahrar ash-Sham denies the accusation, and it is notable that the IF-led March 2014 Lattakia offensive has (so far) been careful to protect Christian and Alawi religious sites and to reassure minority communities. This suggests that a much more disciplined IF has understood how damaging sectarian atrocities are to the revolution. The Front's charter guarantees the protection of religious minorities; revolutionaries from minority communities, meanwhile, have pointed out that talk of 'protection' undermines equality of citizenship. It is also true that Zahran Alloush has spoken of 'cleansing Damascus of Shia influence'. This may mean ending the Syrian state's alliance with Shia Iran. Syrian Shia, Alawis and Ismailis are more likely to read it as a threat of ethnic cleansing.

So the Islamic Front's position on sectarianism remains ambiguous, to say the least. It has certainly fought alongside forces that are more overtly and violently sectarian, such as JaN and even (though far less often, and not at all since January 2014) ISIS. More secular Free Army formations have also fought alongside these Salafist extremists. The reality is that the moderate rebel forces have had no other option. They do not operate within self-selected circumstances – as already noted, the lack of material support for the moderate rebels has led to the over-representation on the battlefield of forces that are not necessarily ideologically popular.

Some supposed rebel forces, such as ISIS, have proven to be not only a major threat to Syria's minorities, but to every single Syrian. Unlike the Islamic Front, ISIS is an overtly counter-revolutionary force – it attacks, imprisons and murders members of rebel factions as much, if not more, than it attacks the Assad regime. ISIS is mostly comprised of non-Syrian jihadis and was formed out of Abu Musab al-Zarqawi's infamous 'al-Qaeda in Iraq', a major element in Iraq's sectarian bloodbath. As a predatory *takfiri* organisation committed only to building its own 'emirate' out of the territory it holds or takes from other rebels, ISIS imposes a strict Wahhabi version of *sharia* on those unfortunate enough to live under its rule, applying capital and corporal punishment against those who defy it. ISIS flourishes due to the fact that it is almost completely self-reliant in terms of weaponry and equipment (from its arsenal in Iraq and gifts from wealthy private donors in the Gulf).

In January 2014, after a series of ISIS attacks on liberated territory, and its capture and execution of a popular rebel commander, coupled with large anti-ISIS protests by residents across the Aleppo governorate, the Free Army in alliance with the Islamic Front launched an offensive against ISIS. While the tactical results of the operation were mixed, with ISIS forced to withdraw from positions in Deir ez-Zor, Lattakia and Idlib, but holding on in Raqqa, the operation was a major victory in terms of showing the Syrian people and the world that the two main rebel forces, the FSA and the IF, were able and willing to take on ISIS in response to civilian pressure. Perhaps the most important political aspect of the action was its demonstration that many within the IF regard ISIS as an enemy of the revolution. It was also the first major offensive involving the newly-formed Syrian Revolutionaries Front (SRF), led by Jamal Maarouf, a coalition of fourteen (more secular) Free Army brigades formed in response to the creation of the IF.

The SRF could be interpreted as the latest attempt by the SMC and the exiled opposition, in collaboration with Saudi Arabia, to prove to the US that there are moderate forces on the ground worth arming and supporting. But it's also possible to interpret it as the coming to the fore of the most self-sufficient Free Army brigades. This doesn't necessarily represent a shift from the exiled opposition's failed strategy of courting US support, but it might indicate an acknowledgement that people such as Maarouf (who, like the IF commanders, successfully built his formation from the bottom up), could serve as some sort of alternative to foreign support.

While the FSA/IF action against ISIS was necessary, it also drained precious resources from fighting the regime. Partly as a result, regime forces backed by Hizbullah and sectarian militias from Iraq managed to recapture the city of Yabroud in March 2014. The consequences of a war on two fronts with no external material support could ultimately draw out the conflict and further embolden Assad in his counter-revolutionary effort.

On 21 August 2013, the regime launched a chemical attack, using the deadly agent sarin, on the opposition-controlled suburbs of Ghouta in Damascus. The world was outraged and the UN was called in to investigate. One outcome was the agreement, crafted by the US Secretary of State John Kerry and his Russian counterpart, Sergei Lavrov, to eliminate Syria's chemical weapons. After the Kerry-Lavrov deal, the US, Russia and the Assad regime began trumpeting the Geneva II peace talks. But the notion that Geneva II could have led to any kind of peace or even any significant gain for the revolution was, at the very least, fanciful. Negotiating with a regime that had managed to turn the tide in its favour on the battlefield was never going to yield results. Assad knows the rebels have been left high and dry by the imperialist powers, and he knows that while he remains able to hold them back, and preserve his massive external support, his domestic base can be maintained and he will have the upper hand in negotiations.

Karl Marx, speaking of the 1853 aggression of the Russian Empire against Turkey, related a parable of two Persian naturalists who come across a bear. The one who has never seen such an animal before inquires whether it gives birth to live young or lays eggs. The other replies: 'that animal is capable of anything.' The savage beast that is the Assad regime is also capable of anything, including using chemical weapons and committing ethnic cleansing on a massive scale, but only because it knows that its enemies are capable of nothing. As long as the imperialist powers of the West continue to block heavy weaponry to the rebels, and refuse to provide such weaponry themselves, as long as Russia and Iran continue to arm the regime, as long as the exiled leadership continues to put all its eggs into the imperialist basket, the Syrian people will continue to pay with their lives, property and freedom.

THE SECT AS HOMELAND

Rasha Omran

On the telephone in Damascus, or via Facebook with Tartus (the Mediterranean coastal city and surrounding region with an Alawi majority, where my home village is located), I caught up with my friends and relatives on the events in Tunisia. We were all gladdened by this extraordinary episode in Arab history. Together we followed news of the Egyptian revolution, hour by hour, as if we were in Tahrir Square ourselves, and together we raised toasts when the end of Hosni Mubarak's presidency was announced. Together we expressed our anger at the brutal violence of Muammar Gaddafi's regime as it launched air strikes on Libyan cities and civilians.

As the revolutions spread from one Arab country to another, we were like a person filled with joy as he witnesses the realisation of a dream he never expected to come true; a great change was occurring to renew the waters of the Arab world which had been muddied and stagnant for a long age.

During this period we used to exchange views on the possibility of the rebellion reaching Syria, where political, economic and social conditions were unsustainable. We were particularly concerned by the lack of public freedoms in the country – freedom of opinion, media freedom, the freedom for political movements and civil society organisations to exist and develop and engage with Syrian society.

My friends, relatives and I shared so much – our ideas, our worries, our dreams too.

Then on 18 March 2011, following the arrest of a group of children who had written the slogans they'd learnt via satellite from other Arab countries ('The People Want the Fall of the Regime!') on the walls of their school, Dara'a province exploded in protest. At the time I was in Morocco, invited to a poetry festival alongside a number of other Arab and African poets. I followed the news on satellite channels and via Facebook, where I kept in touch with my younger daughter and friends throughout Syria. Starting with the fall of the first martyr, I began to write against a security response to the protests and against violence on my Facebook page. I wrote from Morocco, and I criticised the regime with no thought for the consequences. My only fear was that this blood spilt in Dara'a would bring nothing behind it but more blood. Libya was burning then, and I watched the developments there, and compared them to Syrian events with trepidation.

I wrote what I wrote on my Facebook page, and it never occurred to me to look at the pages of my friends and relatives in Tartus to see their reactions to the repression. As far as I was concerned, it was obvious that they would share my ideas and opinions. That's why I didn't bother to look. In any case, I was busy following the news, and checking my daughter's page every day, and constantly warning her not to attend any demonstration until I returned. I remembered well the day we had participated in a demonstration of solidarity with the Libyan people outside Gaddafi's embassy in Damascus, how the Syrian security forces surrounded us on all sides, how they abused and humiliated us in the streets in full view of all, and how they arrested some young men and women. My daughter was with me that day, and she was trying to provoke the security men with slogans such as 'He Who Kills his People is a Traitor' and 'He Who Oppresses his People is a Traitor.'

On the morning of my return to Damascus, 25 March, my daughter and a group of her friends joined a protest in the Hamidiya Souq in the city centre. She was arrested in the heart of the demonstration. I read the news of her arrest on Facebook.

For some days I lived with a fear unlike any I'd known before. I recalled every story I'd ever read or heard of the misery inside Syrian prisons. I was certain I wouldn't be seeing my daughter for a long time.

I didn't bother checking the Facebook pages of my friends and relatives in Tartus that day either. I didn't bother checking to see what they made of my daughter's arrest because I assumed they'd be the first to stand in solidarity with her, especially as her name had been mentioned, coupled with mine, on more than one Arab satellite channel.

You could say that my attention was first drawn to the problematic qualities of Syrian society by my daughter's arrest and then release from prison, and by the comments of my family in Tartus on her experience and on the Syrian situation in its entirety. My daughter told me that the officer in charge of investigating her – a man, like us, from Tartus – when he had worked out who she was, asked her, 'Why did you demonstrate against the regime which protects you?'

'Protects me!' she retorted. 'A regime which arrests children like me! Which murders Syrians!'

'Yes,' the officer said. 'The regime is here to protect Alawis like you.'

He repeated the same line several days later when he called to tell me to pick up my daughter from the security branch. Of course, it was exceptional for them to call a relative in order to hand over someone detained at a demonstration; the exception was perhaps made on account of the cultural authority of my name, or perhaps simply on account of our membership in the Alawi sect, according to their way of thinking. In those days the regime's operatives still cared about their reputation in the eyes of the Syrians first and the international community second. Perhaps they calculated that the arrest of an Alawi girl from a well-known family, a girl who had participated in a peaceful demonstration, would raise uncomfortable questions in quarters where such questions had previously been suppressed.

This was my first direct collision with the notion of 'identity', according to which my daughter and I constitute part of 'Us', the power which protects its followers, a power we must follow simply because we share the sect of its leaders. According to this notion, citizenship enjoys the status of a fallen woman, belonging to the larger homeland means nothing at all, and security must stem from the narrowest sectarian allegiance. The reason for my shock was not that I had previously been deluded enough to believe the regime was patriotic. I was one of those who knew the nature of its political and security structures, and I thought of it as a mafia enterprise surpassing sectarian identity, one that would do anything to maintain its dominance. But I never imagined that its destruction of the country would bring Syria to such a low point. I believed that Syrian society, despite everything, was coherent and strong enough in its depths to withstand any crisis. But the ruination of the last years has revealed an enormous national weakness. This was my second, and more serious, collision with the notion of 'identity'.

One day after my daughter's release I was reflecting with amazement on the fact that only a very few of my friends and relatives in Tartus had contacted me. Indeed, I realised that nobody at all had called to enquire or console during the period of my daughter's detention. It seemed to me a mysterious sign, so I finally opened the Facebook pages of my people in Tartus. I was astounded by what I saw. In most cases their profile pictures had been replaced by images of Bashaar al-Assad or his father Hafez.

I was shocked by their symbolic identification with the regime. This represented a radical transformation, and one which had happened in a remarkably short span of time. People needed more time to consider what was happening in the country before identifying with anything so wholeheartedly. More than that, the blood flowing in Syrian streets had been spilt by the regime. In such circumstances it was everybody's duty to construct their 'identity' from universal morals and humanity – or so I thought, and so I assumed my friends and relatives would also think.

When I write 'my friends and relatives' I mean a very specific slice of the Alawi community. My village, al-Malaja in rural Tartus, is considered one of the best educated in the province despite it being very small, with a population of no more than eight hundred people. Most of these have completed their further education, and include doctors, engineers and lawyers as well as writers, musicians and artists. More importantly, over the last decades the village has witnessed a political and cultural movement and a diverse social openness which was very progressive for the context in time and place. No inhabitant of the village worked for the security services or in the military. Indeed, throughout its history al-Malaja has been categorised (in security terms) as one of the oppositional Alawi villages, and an object of permanent surveillance. I thought the village's exceptional qualities would protect it from the moral landslide apparent in other villages of the region, and indeed among most Syrians, who continued to collude in silence or to openly praise the regime, either out of fear or self interest. However, the destruction of the country and its social fabric was far greater than I had expected. My village could not withstand the damage.

I was by no means the only Alawi to oppose the regime's brutality and to dissent from its sectarian narrative. Journalist and novelist Samar Yazbek, for instance, faced a campaign of vilification and death threats, and was publicly disowned by her family and ancestral village, when she wrote in support of democracy and against state propaganda. Alawi actress Fadwa Suleiman spent the winter of 2011/2012 in besieged Homs, in solidarity with the mainly Sunni inhabitants surviving under bombs. Some Alawis have joined the Free Army and local coordination committees, and others work in secret to deliver food and medicine to their besieged neighbours. But a clear majority of Alawis oppose the revolution and believe the regime line.

I signed the first statement issued inside Syria against the lies of the regime narrative concerning events in Dara'a. The statement and the names of the co-signers were transmitted by Arab and foreign news channels. It was at this point that I became fully aware of the radical change in my friends and relatives. I received several phone calls making various accusations – the greatest of which was treason, the least of which was stupidity.

After I signed the statement, the cultural elite began to boycott me. As I wrote more for the Arab press, and as my Facebook page commentary rose in temperature, the boycott became an attack. A long dictionary of insults was heaped upon me, along with death threats and promises of annihilation. Vicious lies and rumours about me were promoted by those who, only a short while earlier, had been among my closest friends. For me this whole experience was shocking – shocking and bewildering, and it provoked questions as to the causes, roots and depths of this behaviour.

The concept of 'minorities' springs from differentiating them from the social totality and inventing narratives of their historical oppression by the majority living in the same places. These narratives of darkness are then reflected in the behaviour of the members of these minorities. They make them build a shell around themselves; they prevent them from direct contact with the other, obstructing marriages and business partnerships. They also foster a sense of superiority as a sort of compensation for the historical oppression they supposedly suffered, and they differentiate them from the majority, which is not preoccupied with such details. Because of its size, a majority community does not live as an integrated and harmonious entity in terms of individual conduct and manners, but rather as various scattered heterogenous communities only connected to each other by religion, sect or ethnicity. On the other hand, the limited numbers of a given minority make it a relatively harmonious or homogenous entity in terms of daily behaviour. This harmony or internal cohesion is what gives the minority its feeling of superiority and high self-esteem, regardless of the social, economic and cultural conditions in which its members may live.

The Alawis compose 12 per cent of the Syrian population. They were originally called Nusairis, after Imam Muhammad ibn al-Nusair al-Nimairi, one of the attendants of the Awaited Imam. The community was designated 'Alawi' by the French, who found it difficult to distinguish the word 'Nusairi' from 'Nasara' or 'Christian'. The Alawis are considered one of the Shia *ghullu* (exaggerating or extremist) sects in Islam because they believe in the divinity of the Prophet Muhammad's cousin and son-in-law Ali ibn Abi Talib and because their religion is an esoteric and Gnostic amalgam of many different religions and cultures. Something else which distinguishes them from other Muslims is the fact that they have no fixed religious authority and no printed books. Their religion is transmitted from generation to generation by word of mouth and via hand-written manuscripts. Like other religious minorities, they have been subjected throughout their history to religious and political persecution by imams who issued fatwas in the service of political power. The fatwas issued by ibn Taymiyya against Alawis, declaring them *kuffar* (unbeliever) and apostates beyond the limits of Islam and making their killing permissible, played a role in forcing them to leave the cosmopolitan cities and to retreat to the mountains in what is now coastal Syria and Lebanon. This forced withdrawal and the fear of fatwas made them a closed-off, self-enclosed people who lived in fear lest their esoteric religion become public knowledge. And like all the people of the countryside and mountains in Syria and throughout the Arab world, the Alawis suffered too from the oppression of the urban classes.

In March 1963 a group of army officers, mostly from the minorities, launched a successful coup in the name of the Ba'ath Party. The coup was led by Salah Jadeed, Muhammad Omran and Hafez al-Assad – all three of them Alawis. It was followed in 1970 by Hafez al-Assad's coup against the coup. He called his new coup 'the Correctionist Movement', and through it he rose to absolute power, either liquidating or imprisoning his previous partners, including the Alawis. At this point, fatwas were issued by the

Shia imam Musa Sadr, based in Lebanon, and by the shaikh of al-Azhar in Egypt, declaring the Alawis to be a branch of Shià Islam and thus – given that the Syrian constitution states the president must be a Muslim – qualified to rule.

There was a gradual change in Alawi behaviour at this point. They became more open to other non-Alawis, they moved to the cities and began the process of assimilation with the other inhabitants either voluntarily or through the demographic policies imposed by Hafez al-Assad. And like any authoritarian regime which seeks to ensure the permanence of its reign, the Assad regime deliberately brought its sect into the governing apparatus by encouraging them – especially the sons of the rugged mountain communities, where extreme poverty, barren land and a lack of development left them no other options – to join either the security services or the army. Inhabitants of the villages surrounding Qardaha, the president's village, were heavily recruited. As the Assad family increased its prominence and political power, more and more young Alawis became involved in the security industry. On the one hand, a military career protected Alawis from the spectre of poverty; on the other, it gave them a new social status with which to distance the spectre of historical persecution.

In the early 1980s, the Muslim Brotherhood launched a campaign of bombings and assassinations. This campaign was coupled with a sectarian dimension that targeted Alawis specifically. The images of these killings remain fresh in Alawi minds. And Hafez al-Assad, assisted by his brother Rifa'at, was able to exploit his battle with the Muslim Brotherhood to reinforce total control over Syrian society. Rifa'at slaughtered many of his Alawi rivals at this time, blaming their assassinations on the Brotherhood. The Assads ruthlessly eliminated any Alawi authority figure that might potentially oppose them.

In February 1982, when fugitive militants holed up in the ancient city of Hama, the regime destroyed the city entirely over the course of eighteen days, killing 40,000 people. The massacre occurred in sight and hearing of a suspiciously silent world. This silence was a criminal collusion shared by most Syrians, who for decades failed to speak out. After the Hama massacre, fear ruled Syria. Hama was where Syria's social fabric began to dissolve.

Syrians noticed this happening but fear prevented them from doing anything to stop it. Fear grew and flourished among the Syrians and crept like a beast among them. Hafez al-Assad expertly nourished Alawi fears by exploiting the violence of the Muslim Brotherhood to nourish their sense of historic victimhood. He encouraged the development of a hidden grudge against the Sunni majority alongside the assumption that every single member of this majority was either a Brotherhood member or sympathiser.

Assad Senior continued to strengthen Alawi power in the security and intelligence sectors while administrative corruption was generalised until it became the rule rather than the exception. Corruption was directly linked to the security agencies, because the authority of the lowliest security officer exceeded that of even a minister. Meanwhile the idea grew among the majority of Syrians that every member of the Alawi community was inevitably a security officer or intelligence man, or related to one. And of course those who did work in the repressive apparatus were sure that their position depended on the president being from their sect.

A further factor that strengthened support for the regime was its early development of the countryside, electrifying villages and building surfaced roads and water pipelines, including in remote Alawi areas where people may have believed they received these blessings from the state simply because they were Alawis. The regime encouraged this 'favoured community' vision amongst Alawis, urging them to pursue higher education, sending many to study abroad at the state's expense, and providing employment opportunities in the bureaucracy. When Alawis believed that social development was offered as a reward for their sectarian identity, they failed to realise that such basic opportunities were their right as citizens of the nation.

Naturally in this scenario the ideal citizen was the citizen closest to the military-security system. Amongst the Alawis as among the other communities, the idea of citizenship gradually diminished only to be replaced by loyalty to sect, family, clan or class. The mass Syrian national identity itself crumbled into sub-national fragments, each in apparent rivalry with the other to seize what opportunities it could. For the Alawis, if the sect provided both identity and privileges, then it became the homeland; an attack on the sect became an attack against the homeland;

defence of the sect was defence of the homeland; sacrifice for the sect was sacrifice for the homeland's sake.

This distorted view of the homeland was reinforced daily by the stagnation calling itself stability that ruled over a Syria in which there was no outlet for political, civil or cultural activity beyond the constraining framework of the official institutions. Such civic activities could have made a qualitative difference to Syrian society, or could at least have lightened the consistency of daily life, which resembled a living death. Had it been permitted, such a civic movement could have provoked a reconsideration of the notion of citizenship. It would inevitably have changed the relationship of Syrians to the homeland and to the rights and duties that the homeland implies, as well as to each other as partners in all the details which make up the construction of our future civilisation. But was such a movement allowed by the tyrannous regime, by the regime which ruled Syria as if it were a family plantation? Naturally the answer is no. Why? Because the regime was well aware that a free cultural movement affirming the values of citizenship would result in revolution at all levels of society, and in the declaration of the regime's downfall. This was the eventuality the regime sought to avoid at all costs, and this is why it preferred a society of competing blocks, each too scared to speak its obsessions aloud.

When Bashaar al-Assad succeeded his father Hafez, there was great optimism. It seemed Bashaar was opening the door a little to civil society, and it was every Syrian's dream that things would begin to change. Many staked their hope on reform coming from the heart of the regime itself, and awaited the declaration of a national committee to study the events of the eighties and their negative consequences. They awaited a new social contract for Syrians on the basis of citizenship and real participation in the homeland.

Of course, they waited in vain. What happened in fact was the total annihilation of the few emergent civil society groups, an increase in the powers of the security agencies, an ever more blatant generalisation of corruption, an increase in favouritism and nepotism, an increase in the exclusion and marginalisation of large sections of Syrian society, and the near-elimination of the middle class.

All this led to a general loss of hope in any change and resignation to the reality of the situation. As far as many Alawis were concerned, the situation was palatable enough so long as their lives were not in danger. But how quickly this changed with the outbreak of the Syrian revolution, when the regime mobilised to counter the challenge by besieging the revolution in specific areas and alienating it from others – stock divide-and-rule methods. At a time of peaceful protest, state media spoke of armed *takfiri* gangs killing soldiers and security agents (those honourable patriots), and of their goal of sectarian war in Syria. Then it launched false-flag operations and spread rumours amongst the Alawis, reminding them with increased intensity of the narrative of historical persecution. The regime also sacrificed some Alawis in areas of sectarian friction in order to frighten the rest into believing that those who claimed to stand for revolution were actually sectarian killers intent on revenge for Hama. Simply put, the regime let loose the monster of fear which had been latent in Alawi minds, and reinforced the link between homeland and sect, and the link between their personal survival and the survival of the sect/homeland. And today the Alawis believe they're fighting against the threat of personal, sectarian and national extinction, and that the other – he of the different sect – is the enemy who targets the homeland (which is inextricably wrapped up with the sect).

It was for this reason that they were shocked by me and others like me who reject the identification of homeland and sect. The 'betrayal' of which they speak is the betrayal of a concept which, as they understand it, is axiomatic and self-evident. Bashaar al-Assad is not important to them personally, but only as a guarantor of the survival of the unified concept of homeland and sect. Their fear of the revolution is fear of a deeply-rooted mental structure, their individual and collective consciousness, being unsettled. They do not consider the men they have sacrificed as fuel for the war of a ruling dynasty but as martyrs in the path of preserving the psychological typology to which they belong; preserving the fixed ideological reference which has been the title of their lives for forty years and which, for once in history, placed them in the front rank.

Of course it goes without saying that the deviations of the revolution, specifically its Islamisation, which has led to the arrival on Syrian land of al-Qaeda and extremism in all the meanings of the word, and the sectarian media discourse that claims revolutionary affiliation – all strengthen their assumptions and increase their defensiveness.

But will they realise the extent of the delusion under which they have lived for so long? Will they understand that the graves of their children, increasing day by day, were nothing but a cheap price for the regime to pay? The regime treated these children as pawns in a game of chess as it fought for its own survival.

Perhaps they will eventually understand. But this will come long after their lives have been transformed into an endless round of funerals and condolences, and after all, Syria has been transformed into a land of cemeteries and death by the crimes of a regime which uses sectarianism as a tool of war.

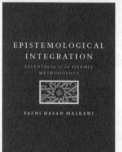

INSIDE AND OUTSIDE

Ella Wind

When it comes to interpreting Syria, a strong tension exists between outside and inside perspectives, between journalistic storylines and anecdotal accounts. This is a tension I've felt deeply through my own experiences, which often seem to stand in stark contrast to traditional narratives about Syria in Western media and academia. I spent six months in Damascus before the overthrow of Egypt's Mubarak. In the short four months after Egypt captured the imaginations of Syrians, I watched my friends in Damascus transform profoundly in their political ideals, aspirations, and even their personalities. In the first year of protests in the country, I often felt that Syria 'experts', who may have had a deep understanding of Syria before the revolution, did not grasp how profoundly it had changed since they undertook their fieldwork. For instance, imagine my bewilderment in the first months of 2011 when I read Syria scholars reiterating that the minorities were scared of the revolution, while I watched my Christian and Alawi friends heading out to the Sunni mosques for Friday protests! I don't mean to dismiss the expertise of a long-term perspective, which I think is certainly valuable. But I want to draw attention to the ways in which, especially in times of rapid and radical societal change, things often look completely different from the inside, and to point out that area scholars aren't always well attuned to the logics of internal dynamics.

One example of an empirical misreading of Syria is the continuing perception from outside of a deep urban-rural divide among the ranks of the opposition. This narrative holds that, until fairly recently, Damascus remained an oasis of quiet untouched by the revolution, partially because the regime was able to successfully squash dissent there by use of force, but also in great part because the urbanised, cosmopolitan citizens of the capital did not want the revolution in the first place. It's easy to see why one would assume this to be the case, based on the scarcity of protests there relative to the rest of the country. In fact, many residents of Damascus were very active protesters – just not in Damascus.

To understand this, we need to soften the overstated analytical division between the urban and the rural in Syria. Many, if not the majority of the people who live in Damascus are only first or second-generation Damascenes, and still identify quite strongly with the town their parents or grandparents came from, and where they may have partially grown up. To be a *Shaami* (Damascene) in Syria implies having a long family history of ties to Damascus, a claim few can make considering the phenomenon of mass migration over the past half-century from the countryside to urban areas. It is not uncommon for Damascus residents to speak two or three distinct Syrian dialects: a standardised Damascus accent, the dialect of where they or their parents grew up, and maybe even the dialect of a parent or grandparent from another rural region. A Syrian who grew up and spent his whole life in Damascus, but whose father was born in Dara'a, would more likely than not identify himself as a Dirawi (of Dara'a).

This means that residents of Damascus, when considering where to protest, did not necessarily have to limit themselves to their neighbourhood in the capital. Many residents, rather than risking *mukhabarat* surveillance and the regime snipers which were posted on rooftops overlooking public areas very early on, chose to participate in protests in the relatively safer spaces of their hometowns. For the same security reasons, many of the protests and much of the organising which took place in the Damascus suburbs and countryside included residents from the inner city. For instance, one of my friends, a woman originally from the town of Yabroud who lived in the capital's Abassiyeen Square, regularly visited Douma in rural Damascus where she helped organise workshops and discussion groups for women. So the journalistic discourse that Damascenes were not protesting seems at first logical, almost tautological, since there were very few protests in Damascus. But this perception is based on a view of rural protests from the outside, without considering the personal life histories and contexts of the protesters, who of course were not stopped and asked what part of Syria they actually lived in.

The discrepancy between journalistic assumptions and reality on the ground is mirrored by the oft-repeated claim that minority groups have not participated in the uprising, a claim evidenced by the fact that protests have mostly occurred in Sunni areas and have usually marched from the mosques. Beginning in 2011, the Christians and Alawis I knew in Damascus began to attend Friday prayers at the city's mosques, specifically in places where they knew protests would occur, as these were the only safe spots where it was feasible to gather people together in large groups. The Damascene equivalents of Tahrir Square almost always had a security branch staffed by armed security personnel located strategically within them, so the Egyptian approach of occupying major public spaces was never a serious option for Syrians. Again, a journalist covering such a protest might surmise that all the people pouring out of the mosque were Sunni Muslims, and naturally would not think to stop to ask a protester coming out of the mosque what religion or sect she belonged to.

Syria remains the biggest surprise of the Arab uprisings. When some isolated protests and vigils took place in early 2011, analysts were quick to point out that Syria was 'not Egypt' and would not likely experience a mass uprising. Indeed, someone visiting Syria before 2011 would have found that Bashar al-Assad did indeed enjoy some degree of real popularity relative to many other Arab leaders such as Hosni Mubarak or Muammar al-Qaddafi. This person, once returned to his own country, might find it hard to imagine that public opinion truly changed course so quickly, and might even believe that the claimed change should be judged as highly suspect. But one aspect of the uprising which remains under-told is the way in which it came as a total surprise even to those who ended up becoming its key figures and organisers on the ground. It wasn't only a surprise to them that an uprising erupted, but also that they found themselves participating in it.

The friends I made when I first arrived in Damascus eventually went on to help organise Local Coordination Committees in Douma, Yabroud, and elsewhere throughout the country. These friends were for the most part architects, archaeologists, and other skilled workers in their late twenties; they were middle class university graduates, and none were originally from Damascus. Because of their occupations, they were deeply involved in community projects. In particular, they often discussed the need for greater public access to the increasingly expensive architectural heritage of the old city, which had started to become accessible only to foreigners with enough money to buy private homes. My friends, however, were almost all explicitly 'apolitical' before the uprising, and would repeatedly mention that fact any time conversations seemed to veer towards the controversial. Even very mundane topics containing key words that could be misconstrued by an eavesdropper were definitively off limits.

There were those rare occasions, sitting in a friend's living room late at night after a few beers, when inhibitions would break down, when other, less taboo topics (relationships, sex, and gossip) had been exhausted, and someone would bring up the Muslim Brotherhood or a Communist uncle who had been long imprisoned. A few might then be willing to venture into this dangerous terrain, offering a commentary, but one of the more sober guests present always knew how to break the mood. A light-hearted joke about the intelligence services ('Hey, the *mukhabarat* should be here any minute you guys, I just texted them!') was enough to steer the conversation back to the acceptable.

At the end of 2010, I had to leave the country to renew my student visa in Lebanon. For Americans, this process took about a month. While I was waiting for my new documents in Beirut, Ben Ali fled Tunisia and protests spread all across Egypt. I came back to Syria in mid-January and went to surprise my friends who were sitting in the Nawfara café, one of the most popular, most crowded cafes in the heart of the old city, and a known favourite for regime eavesdroppers. I said hello and joined the group. It only took a few minutes for me to realise that something had shifted since I'd left. My 'apolitical' friends were loudly cracking jokes about Mubarak and Egypt, with strangers all around us. I remained silent. Scolding them to stop seemed riskier than letting them continue, and they went on candidly opining on protests in Egypt and Tunisia for the rest of the night. My confusion continued into the following week, as variations of this event were repeated. I didn't realise until later on that what I had experienced were the first cracks in the so-called 'wall of fear.' These cracks didn't become visible to the outside world until months later, but they had taken firm root all across the capital even before Mubarak had left office.

Ask any Syrian what his first protest was like, and you receive an almost universal answer: there was a moment of incredible exhilaration, when he felt himself 'free' for the first time in his life. The vast majority of people I have talked to describe it as the single greatest moment of their life. Over and over again, you hear the same description: the tight chest and hands numb from anxiety as he decided to go, as he entered the *service* bus in the morning, and as he walked to the mosque or the square. Then the replacement of the fear by a rush of adrenaline when he first joined in with the singing and chanting. Together they sang '*janna janna janna, wallah ya watanna*' ('paradise, paradise, our country is a paradise'). The chanting, singing and dancing was so thrilling it was almost like a drug, an emotional experience to be sought out again and again. The dream of the next opportunity to go out in the streets consumed his thoughts.

This is a point which has been missed in many journalistic and academic accounts: the way in which, in the course of a few months, small events did irreparable damage to the lifelong training Syrians had received in self-censorship. These little moments came to politicise thousands of Syrians who previously would have declared that they were not 'political people.' It feels strange now when I bring up with friends the things they said to me before or during the first months of 2011. Their statements or reactions in those times are so different to the opinions they hold now that they often take a while to recognise that they actually said them. On a related note, it's also striking, indeed almost humorous, to recall how events or declarations which would now be considered tame or even pro-regime, seemed shockingly bold at the time. This is why statements which could have landed you in jail in 2010 can now be heard coming from the mouths of pro-government figures in attempts to seem 'reasonable' or 'fair.'

But it was not just positive experiences – the thrill of protest and laughing at political jokes in public – that transformed the Syrian consciousness. Accumulating disappointments with the regime as it revealed its true face and intentions transformed into anger. The nonchalant dismissal by Assad of the people's suffering, the arrests of friends and family members and an inexorably expanding awareness of the grim reality of Syrian prisons, as well as the deaths of popular and beloved civil society figures, all contributed to the rapid downturn in Assad's popularity. No conspiracy theory is required to make sense of the speed with which Assad went from being one of the most popular leaders in the Arab world to being so despised by his own people.

A few months after my return to Syria, Bashaar al-Assad delivered his first speech since the beginning of the protests. I was at a friend's house, and we ran downstairs to watch it, crowded with his roommates around the tiny TV in the living room. At this point, dozens of protesters had been killed by security forces but the president had still made no comment. Many if not most of the Syrians I knew still hesitantly put trust in the oft-repeated slogan 'the president is good, but those around him are bad.' This essentially meant that Assad had good intentions for the country, but the inner circle around him was corrupt and prevented him from moving forward. There was a sense at the time among the tentatively pro-Assad crowd, therefore, that the momentum of the protests had opened up a space for Bashaar to push forward with his 'long-awaited' reforms, even if his inner circle had been pushing security forces to repress protesters. There was a great expectation, even palpable excitement, that of course Assad would apologise for the killings and introduce reforms.

The president's speech was long and circumlocutory. It wasn't quite clear where it was going, but the room's sense of happy expectation deflated further with each mention of 'enemies' and 'conspiracy'. Then the speech finished rather abruptly.

Everyone in the room was quiet, looking at each other silently. One eventually broke the silence: 'That's it?' Nothing more needed to be said. The shock was tangible. Many of the people I watched this first speech with later became very active organisers of the opposition.

As it became clearer that Assad was fully aware of the scale of the repression, it became more difficult to shift the blame onto a corrupt inner circle that could be dismissed by the president. Instead, every arrest of a neighbour, every burn mark on the chest of a friend returning from prison, was personified as the work of Assad and his total refusal to accommodate even the most peaceful voices of the growing opposition. One such voice was that of Bassel Shahadeh, a young filmmaker from the Qassa neighbourhood of Damascus.

I first met Bassel through the *Maseer* group, a loose network of people who met up every month in a predetermined place to go hiking, camping, and to explore Syria's diverse wilderness. The people who took part in *Maseer* were of all occupations, sects, ethnicities, and from various regions. Bassel's curly hair and freckles made him seem much younger than his twenty-seven years. But undoubtedly the most striking thing about Bassel beyond his friendly demeanour was how political he was. Before I'd left for

Lebanon, Bassel was the only Syrian I'd met who was unafraid to speak candidly – not only about politics and corruption, but on other social taboos too. Every year, there's a spat of silly bickering on social media about the 'start of the revolution,' as if there were a precise date in March to pin on the calendar, as if the protests of 2011 were born on one specific day, and were not the result of a build-up over the preceding months, years, and decades. I always find this bickering especially strange because in my mind there's one particular date that no one else talks about, much less probably remembers.

On a drizzly day, 28 January, two months before women in Dara'a marched in front of the police station demanding the release of their imprisoned sons, Bassel and a small group of friends lit candles together. They stood in front of the Egyptian embassy in Damascus and called for solidarity with the protesters occupying Tahrir Square. That day it was all anyone in Damascus could talk about, but still in whispers and only with close friends. The rumours and jokes said that more *mukhabarat* attended the vigil than genuine activists. The action ended after a few hours, and Damascus released a collective breath, whether of disappointment, anticipation or relief. Syria would never be Egypt, everyone agreed. Tahrir Square would never happen here.

Bassel's political commitments lay not only in criticising authoritarianism in his country, but in a belief that war is hell, and that the only way to build a just society was through non-violent activism and civil disobedience. His film work reflected this stance. When we later met up in Damascus again, he asked me to watch the movie he was using in his application for a Fulbright scholarship to a US film school. The film, 'Saturday Morning Gift', was based on a conversation he had with a Lebanese boy on his memories of the 2006 Israeli-Lebanese war. One of his first films, 'Carrying Eid to Camps', followed a group of young Syrian volunteers who brought Eid gifts and aid to refugees displaced by the drought in Eastern Syria.

Bassel had called openly for free Syria years before others could even whisper it to themselves in private. But he had other dreams too. He'd waited patiently for a chance to attend film school. And then both dreams seemed to come true at once. He soon heard that he'd won the Fulbright to study in the United States. But when Syrians began to protest in March,

Bassel immediately devoted all his time to working with the grassroots opposition groups that began to take form around Damascus. He trained many other activists in filmmaking, and these went on to document important events of the uprising. In July 2011, Bassel participated in a protest of artists and intellectuals, and was detained for three days. A month after his arrest, when the momentum of the uprising seemed to be at an all-time peak, he left Syria to attend Syracuse University.

He tried to find ways to channel his frustrated energy as he watched events unfold at home from a small city in upstate New York. He spent many nights at the Occupy encampments there and in New York City. Most of all, he put his energy into producing a film to encourage his fellow Syrians to continue along the path of non-violent civil disobedience. For his uncompleted film *Singing to Freedom*, he interviewed leftist intellectuals in the US such as Noam Chomsky, Norman Finkelstein, and Amy Goodman, and he also interviewed his friends back home, such as human rights lawyer Razan Zaitouneh, as they expressed solidarity with the Syrian revolution and urged continuing civil disobedience. The film also features clips of some of the most powerful and cleverest protest songs and chants from Syria. Yet this work never satisfied the urge he felt to be present in the revolution he had long awaited. He left for Syria during his winter break, and never returned to the United States.

Bassel spent the next few months training more activists in filmmaking. He mostly stayed in Homs, nicknamed 'the Capital of the Revolution', to document the various civil initiatives there and the violence of the siege imposed by the regime. During the media blackout in the aftermath of the horrific Houla massacre on the outskirts of Homs, he went to the site to conduct interviews. On 28 May 2012, he was killed in Homs during a government assault.

When they heard the news of his death, some of my friends went to mourn at a church near his house in Damascus. Security agents invaded the church and warned those present to leave. The mourners assembled in a private home, but again they were surrounded, and soon checkpoints were set up in the streets of the area to prevent anyone from commemorating Bassel's death. Several friends who were inside the church were arrested and detained for months.

Bassel's death made waves across Syria. I admit I wasn't aware of how well known he was until after he died. The killing of Bassel and others like him undermined the faith of those who wanted to believe that the regime was only targeting armed terrorist groups – what did it mean? Was Bashaar al Assad threatened even by a condolence ceremony for a young filmmaker who preached against violence?

In war-shattered Syria, activists and ordinary citizens are menaced not only by the regime but also by new forms of authoritarianism, the most extreme of which is the al-Qaeda breakaway group, the Islamic State in Iraq and Syria (ISIS). Opposition to ISIS, and an impressive new coordination between more moderate opposition militias, has pushed the group out of many of its former strongholds in the north and east. This move against ISIS is understood by many as a second liberation, for towns invaded by ISIS were returned to the pre-revolutionary reality of frightened whispers, as its (mainly foreign) fighters arrested and killed popular civil society leaders.

ISIS sees people like Father Paolo Dall'Oglio as an anathema. An Italian Jesuit priest, he has lived in Syria for many decades working for cross-religious cooperation. He is loved and accepted by Syrians as one of their own, and during the revolution he became a leading figure of the opposition. Exiled by the regime, he spoke internationally on the revolution's behalf before returning to the liberated north of Syria, where he was eventually abducted by ISIS. Father Paolo's detention was one of the earliest signs that ISIS should not be considered part of the opposition, but was a danger to one of the most popular opposition figures in Syria.

I first met Father Paolo on an Orthodox Easter weekend. I had driven, with some friends, north from Damascus to Deir Mar Mousa (the Monastery of Saint Moses), which is carved into a mountainside deep in the desert. The only way to the top is up over 300 steps. The church dates back to the sixth century, and its original frescoes are still preserved. It was abandoned, but Paolo renovated it in the 1970s as a monastery and centre for both Christian and Islamic studies and Muslim-Christian dialogue. In addition to his Jesuit training, Paolo studied Islamic theology extensively and speaks fluent Arabic. Deir Mar Mousa attracts small groups of travellers of all religions and sects from Syria and throughout the world, who come to stay and eat for free in exchange for help with cooking and cleaning.

For Arab Christians, Easter holds a deeper religious significance and is a far more elaborate holiday than Christmas. We spent Good Friday doing the Stations of the Cross, wandering into the mountains with a wood carving of Christ, going through the condemning to death up until his placing in the tomb, while different people took turns reading the relevant passages from the Bible. On Holy Saturday, we spent a quiet day resting, just as Christ 'rested' in the tomb.

Finally that night the figurine of Christ was wrapped in a white shroud in the centre of the church, and people filed up to kiss his head and lay the flowers they had collected in the mountains. Then Paolo began his sermon. He wished safety for the President, as the church was required to do by the regime minders who were popping in periodically. I saw a friend wince out of the corner of my eye. By that time, 200 people had been killed and the traditional Easter processions in Syria had been cancelled to respect those who had died.

Paolo then began to preach of the sacrifice Christ had made for forgiveness and for peace. He went on to speak of the slain brothers and sisters in Dara'a and other parts of Syria, who had also given their lives for a greater cause. This was the first time I'd heard someone talk about the victims so openly from such a public forum. Most of those in attendance were weeping. It felt incredibly powerful that day to witness such an important figure speaking out, and even more so because the platform belonged to a religious group which the media claimed would never criticise the regime. In fact, one year and one month later, after tens of thousands more deaths, Paolo's last act before leaving Syria was to preside over the funeral in Homs of Bassel Shahadeh, who also happened to be a Christian.

After the service, we went to sleep. At midnight, we were woken up and returned to the church. The dark mood from Christ's 'burial' on Saturday still hung over the room. But during the service the mood changed to one of joy. The liturgical music became dance music, and the monks and Paolo began to call out '*Qam al-Maseeh, haqqan qam!*' (Christ is risen, verily he is risen!). Soon everyone was dancing and kissing each other's cheeks. Those who hadn't been able to pull themselves out of bed continued to file into the church throughout the night, until we were all crowded together inside, where we stayed until dawn. The celebration held an enormous sense of optimism for the coming months in Syria, and I think a sense too that those who had died would be honoured by what was to rise from their sacrifice.

I had to leave Syria suddenly three days later. Soon afterwards, Paolo released an open letter demanding a peaceful transition to democracy in Syria. He met with opposition activists and issued public statements condemning the deaths and imprisonments of Syrian dissidents. He was answered with an expulsion order from the regime. Despite this, he remained in Syria until May 2012 when, at the urging of his bishop, he left for Iraqi Kurdistan.

In the summer of 2013, Paolo returned to Syria. He wanted to serve as a voice for peace between opposition groups, and he entered rebel-held territory in eastern Syria to work on mediating between different rebel bands and Local Coordination Committees. He was reported to be going to the ISIS headquarters in Raqqa, to enter into good faith negotiations with the hope of ending the antagonistic stance ISIS had taken against all rebel groups not in line with their narrow ideology. Paolo never returned. His whereabouts and status are unknown.

Paolo's disappearance and the subsequent revelation that ISIS was responsible made waves around and outside Syria via social media. For many who had not yet decided what to make of ISIS, this event was transformative. If the group was willing to arrest – even kill – Father Paolo, who wouldn't they stop at? Protests broke out in Raqqa, and spread across Eastern Syria and finally the whole country. The slogan spray-painted and retweeted so many times '*wayn abuna paolo?*' ('Where is our Father Paolo?') made this new perspective clear.

Syria today seems to offer nothing but despair. But perhaps there is reason for optimism in this one observation: the new culture of protest, the refusal to be intimidated into silence, the conviction that legitimate rule can only arise from the choice and consent of the people and not by force of arms – all this is directed not only against the regime, but at any power which attempts to enforce authoritarian policies in Syria.

So long as Syrians are reminded of what changed their minds in the first place – the flippant dismissal and fierce repression of protests, the imprisonment and killing of dissidents, and the heavy-handed stifling of critical thought – they recognise these behaviours not only in the cloak of Ba'athism, but the Islamist variants too. Syria's future looks bleak, admittedly – so much has been destroyed, so many have been killed, and no one knows when this long nightmare will end. But one thing has changed for the best and for ever: Syrians are no longer willing to be humiliated into silence.

THE BRA IN ALEPPO

Malu Halasa

Aleppo is an ancient city, quite possibly the oldest settled metropolis in the world. According to one theory, Aleppo derives its Arabic name, Halab (from milk – *haleeb*), from the milky white sheep that the Prophet Ibrahim tended in the region. It has a long history of textile production, thanks to its strategic location at an ancient crossroads of trade and empire. Syria was also blessed with ready supplies of linen, wool and cotton from as early as the Iron Age. Strategic location and an abundance of raw materials combined with the legendary Syrian talent in looming and weaving encouraged a flourishing textile industry.

Aleppo became a key station along the Silk Road from China and Central Asia to the West either overland, via Iraq and Persia, or by sea across the Indian Ocean, and then via Basra and Baghdad. Rome acquired almost all its silk from Syria. Shakespeare often mentions Aleppo in his plays as an alluring and powerful city. His contemporary, the English merchant Ralph Fitch, reported his travels to Aleppo and beyond over the period 1583–91. One classic blend of wool and silk, often cast in a distinctive fabric with stripes running lengthwise, is called *alepin* after the city of its creation, and is still popular today. During the late eighteenth century the French traveller Comte de Volney described Ottoman Aleppo as the chief entrepôt for trade with Turkey and Armenia. Until the early nineteenth century Aleppine trade with Europe was as important as with the surrounding Middle East. As a result of all this enterprise, Aleppo acquired the largest warren of covered *suqs* (markets) in the world, running to 13 km in length. The covered markets were home to a number of legendry *suqs*, such as Suq Khan al-Wazir, for cotton products; the sixteenth century Suq Harir, for silk; and possibly the largest, the Suq Khan al-Gumrok, built in 1574, originally a customs centre, now home to fifty-five textile stores. The *medina*, or Old City, also contained numerous re-utilised *khans* (trading inns or caravanserais) and these spawned a centuries-old yet often affectionate rivalry with the *khans* in the country's capital, Damascus.

Throughout the past decades, Syrian manufacturing remained resilient, greatly aided by a cotton industry ranked eleventh in the world—one place behind Egypt. In fact, it could be argued that textiles long provided a link to the global economy for a country which in other respects seemed like an island unto itself. For many years, Syria was a magnet for companies such as Benetton, Naf Naf, Stefanel, Kickers and Adidas, and billboard hoardings advertising local textiles and clothing alongside Hyundai cars and Sony electronics littered the highway to Aleppo. But in case the wrong impression was given, that capitalism was king, an enormous portrait of Hafez al-Assad overlooked the first of the city's major roundabouts.

The fact that the capital had become the bastion of the Alawi minority that has effectively ruled the country, through the Assad family, since the 'Corrective Movement' of 1970, was a particular source of grievance for Aleppo. Aleppine feathers had been ruffled already in 1958 when Egypt and Syria formed the United Arab Republic, a pan-Arab experiment that ended in 1961. Towards the very end of that period, in July 1961, Egyptian President Gamal Abdel-Nasser nationalised Syrian industries. The factories of Aleppo's industrial families were confiscated, and many left the country for freer business environments. Syria seceded from the UAR when army officers seized power in September. Two years later another army coup appointed a Ba'athist cabinet, and in 1966 an Alawi-controlled military wing of the Ba'ath ('Renaissance' or 'Renewal') Party began its authoritarian rule. But despite periodic setbacks, the city continued its manufacturing tradition.

Although Aleppo is incredibly ethnically diverse, Sunni Arabs still make up the majority of the city's population. When I visited in 2005, the relatively few uncovered women on the city's streets gave the initial impression that a headscarf was compulsory. Yet, consistent with the distinction between public and private, interior spaces were more revealing. According to Palig Avakian, an athletic thirty-five-year-old Armenian woman who was a customer service representative for Areeba, the country's second-largest mobile phone company, Aleppo was filled with hundreds of women-only gyms and sports halls where women of all religions mixed freely. These were the new *hammams*. She herself trained three times a week and boxed. 'As a woman, I can enjoy my body and veiled women can enjoy their bodies too,' she said.

The history of trade in silk, damasks, brocades and other textiles, as well as the legacy of traditional garb, like the male headgear, the *keffiyeh*, or the female *hijab*, is well documented since at least the Abbasid period. In contrast, we know little about the history of Syrian lingerie manufacturing. Nihad Tabbakh, who owned a lingerie shop in the labyrinth of Aleppo's Old City, dated the tradition of buying and collecting of racy lingerie among working-class Muslims for their wedding night to the *Tishrin* or October War. In 1973 Syria and Egypt launched a surprise attack against Israel and caught it off guard during the Jewish holiday of Yom Kippur. Although the Israelis eventually pushed back the Arab armies, the October War was considered a victory in the Arab world compared to the fiasco of the 1967 Six-Day War, when Syria lost the Golan Heights. After 1973, Gulf countries, appreciative of Assad's prowess, invested in Syria, and luxuries like lingerie began to circulate. Tabbakh remembered: 'We were at war, and you cannot celebrate when you're afraid. After a war that we supposedly won, there were many weddings, and women began to wear sexy lingerie.'

Hanging from the walls of his tastefully laid-out store were examples of women's marriage nightwear ranging from delicate scoop-neck satin nightdresses to sheer, two-piece affairs, some with a red bib-like top and flared trousers trimmed with alternating ruffles and boa feathers. A doctor friend of Tabbakh's visiting the shop suddenly excused himself, saying he was in a hurry to get to the mosque for midday prayers. Within minutes, Tabbakh's co-worker opened a Qur'an on the store counter and began reciting under his breath. Tabbakh, in his sixties, had performed the Hajj. A former teacher himself, he gave discounts to teachers getting married. He described a bride-to-be, usually accompanied by her mother and aunts, coming to his store and picking out lingerie for the first night of her marriage: 'The young ones are rather embarrassed. According to Islamic ideals, a woman must stay at home so she cannot be in touch with men, but she wants to be happy and show her husband that she has something special. Sometimes they mention that they are looking for thirty colours for thirty different things. She wants many colours because maybe her husband likes one colour better than another. She doesn't yet know his feelings.'

In spite of the perception that only Muslim women were prevented from getting to know the men they were supposed to marry, young, traditional Christian women were also segregated. In both religions, the families vetted suitable candidates, but even after the official engagement there was a good chance the couple never met without supervision. While a woman's virtue is lauded in Islam, it has become a defining factor throughout polite Syrian society—the difference between being marriageable and unmarriageable. Sexual purity serves as capital for a young woman; and its absence ruins a young woman's potential prospects.

The evolution of women's undergarments in Syria followed a similar trajectory to those in the West: social change created new styles, except the pace had been slower in Syria due to the country's political controls. The bra, essentially a Western invention, came relatively late to Aleppo. Its evolution began in 1900s France, with the gradual phasing out of the corset and the introduction of modern elasticised fabrics by the 1930s. As European women became more athletic, the emphasis of their underclothing changed from restriction to support. Some say that World War I had an effect as well, by emphasising a need for practicality, and by bringing newfound freedoms for European women, of which the bra was arguably a symbol or a by-product. By the 1940s Arab aristocracy knew about the bra and glamorous nightwear. The Arab world had its own version of cinematic glamour, captured in the classic Egyptian films of the 1950s and 1960s, and the pervasiveness of the high style was encapsulated not only in the portraits of celebrities but also of ordinary Egyptians by the studio photographer Van Leo (1921–2000). The bra, an essential item for the new woman, reached other countries in the Middle East first, and was not mass-produced in Syria for working-class consumption until as late as the 1970s. At Shenineh, one of the city's oldest cotton wear manufacturers, its rise was charted.

The Shenineh factory started with cotton yarn and ended up producing 4,000 pieces of women's camisoles, thongs and G-strings, plus men's briefs and t-shirts destined for the Middle East and Europe. Its office was located near Khan al-Wazir, the *suq* with a beautiful black-and-white marble façade built between 1678 and 1682. Shenineh gave the impression of global cool, from its tastefully wood-panelled shop to its stylish brochures and pamphlets for prospective foreign clients.

Yasser Shenineh, the thirty-five-year-old son who ran the business with his father and brother, explained that the factory manufactured illegal goods for seven years before it received its official license from the government in 1963. For the first twenty-five years, it produced three styles of classic men's t-shirts for the Soviet Union, then the main market for Aleppine clothes. By the 1980s European brands realised Syria was a source of good, cheap cotton, and Shenineh was contracted by French, German and Italian firms to manufacture more modern styles. During this period, Hafez al-Assad also lifted certain restrictions on the country, and people were exposed to foreign influences. The domestic market clamoured for more variety in underwear styles at home. 'Women no longer wanted big panties that came to the waist,' recalled Shenineh. 'By 1987 they weren't asking for the 'string' [the thong], but they were looking for something pretty.'

He summoned the company's oldest employee to join us. Abu Ali Selah al-Din Bella, sixty-four, had been working for Shenineh since the factory's illegal opening. A tall, lanky man with glasses, he seemed an unlikely commentator on the developments in Arab women's underwear. However, like many traditional Middle Eastern husbands who did the shopping for the women at home, he had been purchasing lingerie for his wife over forty years. He remembered the way women in the old days used to strap up their breasts, in thick elasticised bands, much like the headbands used under the *hijab* today. If they were not strapping up their breasts, they wore garments that resembled a full-length slip, called a *shel-ha*.

The top half was embroidered and the skirt finished with an elasticised hem. From the 1940s to the 1960s this garment stayed essentially the same, except it was shortened to keep pace with changing hemlines; in the modern version of the *shel-ha* the traditional elasticised hem had been replaced by a simple embroidered border. In the 1970s Abu Ali's wife started wearing a bra. He says she preferred it because of the size of her breasts. 'When she didn't wear one, they moved inside her clothes like small animals.' Every generation had its own style. Instead of plain white bras, his wife asked him to now bring home rose-coloured ones.

The company's well-produced camisoles and briefs for women and Y-fronts for men could be easily sold in any Western department store. 'We know our product and our product is good. Where we fail is in marketing,' said Shenineh. He admitted taking Calvin Klein imagery off the Internet to use in his brochures. Shenineh sometimes hired Lebanese models to mimic Calvin Klein poses but it was not the same. The company would never resort to the Eastern European models who model racy lingerie in Damascus, he explained, because it would send the wrong message to their customers. Still, pictures of semi-naked Eastern European women graced the windows of lingerie shops in Aleppo's Old City. There was an implicit understanding that their lack of attire did not matter because they were not Muslim or Arab. In the world of sexy lingerie that is mainly produced, manufactured and marketed in Damascus, Syrian women never model. However in Aleppo, an even more conservative city, some women went against family and religious values and did model.

Amongst the first local models was Amal Muhammad. She worked for Issa Touma, a photographer and curator of Le Pont, Aleppo's only gallery for contemporary photography. Le Pont was known for showing 'all things scandalous—pieces by Jewish artists, portraits of nude men and women, videotaped performance art verging on the pornographic—none of it submitted to government censors for approval.' Amal came from the Syrian coast to attend university in Aleppo. Away from her family, she made the decision to forgo the veil. Amal, Touma pointed out, was making an interesting transition, one he had witnessed in other Muslim women friends he had photographed. In conservative Syrian cities and towns, living without the veil required a steeliness of character. Another model made the decision to unveil, and wouldn't give her new address to her family because they had started to threaten her. For some traditional, observant families, forgoing the *hijab* in public was radically unacceptable.

Touma is of Armenian origin, like many Middle Eastern photographers, from Jerusalem to Isfahan, who have documented social changes in the region. Self-taught, he pushed boundaries and became a controversial figure in his country. From 1996 to 2001, he earned a significant part of the operating budget for Le Pont from his advertising work for Aleppo's cotton lingerie companies. He photographed Lebanese models for Shenineh. For its rival, Hanin, he worked with the Brazilian model

Claudia. Those photographs, sometimes including the odd male model—the most memorable featured Claudia in bras and a bridal veil and her Syrian male counterpart, Wael, in a bow tie and shorts, celebrating a cotton lingerie wedding—were taken in the main room of Le Pont, where Touma rigged up a studio set with a white backdrop and ceiling lights. Claudia, a professional, eventually became the Hanin poster girl, and her photographs decorated the walls of dedicated Hanin shops all over Syria. With Amal, Touma decided to be more daring. When he told Hanin company executives of his plans to do a lingerie shoot outdoors, they became nervous. Few Aleppine photographers were as bold as Touma, and although he had gotten away with photographing nudes and exhibiting the photos in Aleppo's Old City, the idea of doing a lingerie shoot in public seemed a recipe for disaster. 'Usually on a shoot, the company sends two women to style the lingerie on the model,' recalled Touma. 'When we shot outside, the only person who came with us was the driver. I'm sure he was told by the owner if there were any problems—just run away.'

Amal was wearing Hanin's cotton camisoles and panties under her clothes when they arrived in the Euphrates River valley an hour outside of Aleppo. She took off her top and pulled down her trousers. In Touma's photographs, her jeans and the top of her stockings could be glimpsed. Although, as he correctly predicted, passers-by stopped and watched, the unschooled model displayed a natural talent. Her inward-looking gaze suggested a woman totally comfortable with her sexuality at a time and in a place where women's sexuality is still considered to be *fitna* ('disorder').

In 2002, a thirty-year ban on private automobile imports was revoked, and the new legislation opened Syria to car imports for the first time since the 1960s. The first ATM machines arrived and the government rescinded a long-held stricture on Syrian citizens trading in foreign currency. In Aleppo, such regulation had a broad brief. The fashion among local industrialists was the building of new factories in the farming countryside of Hayyan, north of the city. Owners often took the opportunity to construct opulent summer villas adjacent to their plants. Few zoning laws existed or, if they did, there were many ways of circumventing them. Aleppo, while the largest city in the Levant, was still comparatively small, with a central population of approximately 2.5 million people. Everyone knew each other's business, especially when it came to bribing government officials.

The majority of Syrian factories were family-owned, and followed a strict hierarchical structure. According to a popular joke, the first-born helped his father with the factory and became his father's right-hand man. He had an office on the first floor. The second son handled the finances and had an office on the second floor. The third was sent abroad to learn English and marketing, and had an office on the third floor. If the factory burnt down, the youngest wouldn't get out alive.

Abdullah Olabi, a third son, was sent to the UK to improve his English and to earn a degree in fashion and business administration for the family-owned Olabi Company Quality Clothing Industries. The Olabi Company, which first made its name in coffee roasting, had diversified. It now manufactured men's and women's cotton briefs and t-shirts, as well as outdoor tents for Saudi Arabia. In 2003, the company had a turnover of USD 6 million due to orders received from Puma, J-Lo, Phat Farm and Baby Phat. Olabi was contracted to make first-rate designs by big name brands that sold all over the world. Yet there was a good chance the people wearing the clothes it produced would not know where Syria was located on a map.

But the Olabi Company's success was short lived. In December 2003, the Syria Accountability Act passed into US law making it illegal for American firms to do business in Syria or import the country's cotton goods. As a result, Olabi lost 60 per cent of its business. The million t-shirts the company was manufacturing yearly shrunk to a mere 200,000–300,000. More detrimental in the long run was Olabi's inability to create t-shirts with a modern, compelling design. In the beginning, friends abroad gave the company designs that Olabi changed by 40 per cent—the percentage needed to avoid a breach of copyright—but that was not enough. Now the sporty brown t-shirt with yellow racing stripes which the twenty-five-year-old Abdullah designed himself and which he was wearing, mapped his company's fortunes since sanctions. His Syrian friends liked the t-shirt because its combination of colours had not been seen in Aleppo's *suq*. But Olabi knew not to wear the t-shirt too much in public, in case someone saw and copied it outright, the predictable outcome of designing any new or remotely profitable garment in Syria.

Olabi's father's underwear line, Extra Tech—plain white men's and women's briefs, t-shirts and men's boxer shorts, similar in style to Fruit of the Loom—sold well in cities like Lattakia and Tartus on the Mediterranean coast, where a population with less disposable income preferred unembellished styles. The factory still manufactured garments with polyester, not nylon (a thread that makes lingerie easier to clean and wear) because of the difficulties of getting special equipment into the country. Olabi admitted that 'Syrian businessmen have difficulties if they try to bring in new technology. It is a political situation and a customs problem in Syria. A new machine can wait at the border. There are many political pressures on businessmen'.

There were social pressures, too. When Olabi first returned from the UK to work in the family firm, he immediately sent the children working in the factory home. Syria was a poor country, and child labour was not uncommon. The land behind Olabi's new factory was turned into grass tennis courts. One of the Olabi-produced tents provided respite for players fried by the country's gruelling summer heat. In the car heading back to town, Olabi complained about the untrained workforce, which has a tendency to move from factory to factory. They refused to contribute to government-run pension schemes into which he, as an employer, must pay by law. That was where he spent his morning, paying the government. There was always something to pay. He admitted that to build his factory in Hayyn he paid a USD 40,000 bribe to the government, which wanted all new factories built in a 'Factory City' on the other side of Aleppo. But the location of the government's new industrial park was poorly chosen. Goods trucks would have had to fight the city's notorious traffic jams before reaching the road to Hayyan and the economic gold fields of Turkey and beyond.

Despite enormous obstacles, it was not Damascus but Aleppo which produced the country's first international underwear brand. A tall order at any time but particularly so in a climate of economic sanctions. Establishing an international brand requires mental and emotional prowess. Everything has to be controlled, from the sourcing of materials, design, manufacturing and marketing of the product, to the environment in which it is sold. In order to be respected, the brand must be consistently displayed at its best advantage. Aleppo's international brand was produced at the Hanin factories.

Hanin belongs to Georges Moussalli, who is also the general director of the company.

In 1860 Moussalli's great-grandfather produced silk in Aleppo. As a child Moussalli lived with his uncle who, after the French Occupation (1920–46), opened a large textile plant, bringing in the best machines from England. When the factory was nationalised in the 1960s, his uncle advised him to pick a profession beyond the reach of politics—something like medicine, because all a doctor needs is a pen for writing prescriptions. Moussalli trained as a civil engineer and still has a civil engineering company, but Hanin remained his true love.

His basement factories were located on quiet city streets. The mirrored walls gave the appearance of larger rooms. Air-conditioning systems and canteens improved conditions for the workers who sat at rows and rows of machines sewing women's panties or camisoles. Sometimes two people at a machine—two men or a man and a woman in a *hijab*—strictly enforced quality control. Good business, Moussalli said, is a negotiation between a proprietor and his workforce.

In his late fifties, he was fully aware of all aspects surrounding his 350-employee company, which had buildings dotted throughout Aleppo. His dedicated Hanin lingerie stores in Syria had the same clean lines and airy spaces as Benetton shops. Hanin sold in France, Germany, Italy and Russia, but as Moussalli quickly stressed, 'we are not just producers of lingerie. We are an international brand. We have our identity, our strategy and our politics. We made our current collection eighteen months ago. We work with the Bureau de la Mode [The Style Office] in Paris and have our French and other international stylists.' He held up the 'Hanin Bible,' in which the company philosophy, related visuals, consumer profiles and marketing strategies had been carefully formulated. The exercise led to the reorganisation of his company, a process he periodically revisited.

Hanin controlled 23 per cent of Syria's women's underwear market. Other companies adopted similar-sounding names to confuse consumers and share the profits. Sometimes the product looked identical. However, in the case of the silk-trim camisole, a staple of Hanin, copiers like Hanri skimped on the measurements and garments were ill-fitting. Syrian women's wear suffered from the lack of standard sizing for women throughout the country's manufacturing industry. Every company invented its own sizes, and sometimes on the wrong shape. Touma told a wonderful story about taking photographs in Aleppo's *suq* in the late 1990s and stumbling into a factory where they were measuring women's lingerie on a Turkish man.

Moussalli knew that women's lingerie was a family affair. Any change involved 'the mother, the husband, the brothers and, let me tell you, they don't like the 'slip" - the thong. 'Today only 15 per cent of the women in Syria want the slip. In Europe 85 per cent of the women want the slip. Although European fashion is popular with some of the young girls here in Aleppo, no more than 5 per cent wear the slip.' Hanin reflected this in its product line. The company did not manufacture stand-alone bras. Instead they integrated them inside their camisoles. The ideal woman customer in Moussalli's estimation was not someone who stayed at home entertaining her husband; she was someone on the go. He did not mean to be insulting, but his assessments were blunt: 'The woman in Syria today is the woman in Europe 100 years ago'. To survive in a business climate like Syria's, Moussalli did business no matter who was in charge of the country. He recalled: 'One day our old president was on TV. He said, now we are in a very bad position, we must tighten our belts. At that point I understood that there was no chance for the borders to open.' The only thing Moussalli and others like him could do was fall back on local resources, and the country started producing practically everything itself, from pharmaceuticals to cars. During this period Moussalli had a contract with C&A, the European clothing store, and managed to produce 1,500 t-shirts a day on five machines built in 1956. When Syrian cotton prices rose and C&A took its business elsewhere, he learned a valuable lesson about self-sufficiency: 'Now everyone says that Syria is no good.' He was referring to international criticism of his country. 'Okay,' he shrugged, 'No problem. We are 18 million people, we can live without.' (The pre-war population was closer to 23 million).

Eleven years after Moussalli started Hanin he introduced the brand to Europe, where he witnessed the rise of Chinese goods at the international trade shows. Lifted at the start of 2005, the quotas set in the WTO Multi-Fiber Agreement on Tariffs and Trade forced Syrian clothing manufacturers to compete on the basis of quality and fashion. Because of the flood of cheap Chinese textiles, the Syrians lost out on price. Another problem came in the form of a free-trade deal that Syria signed in 2004 with Turkey, a vast market just 50 km north of Aleppo. Cheap Turkish clothes imports hit Aleppo's industries hard.

Despite the obstacles, Moussalli remained a businessman willing to gamble on a good idea. 'Now in Europe, men's underwear is important. For the past twenty-five years, men wore 'classic' briefs. But today men are like women. They want something sexy, different. This is important to us now because nobody wants to make this underwear in the Middle East or China. I know there's money in this box.'

In the Middle East, women's clothing has always been a prism of social transformation. In *Islamic Textiles*, Patricia L. Baker traces changes in women's tailoring during the Mandate period, after the arrival of uniformed British and French troops in Palestine. Just as frilly, airy things by Prada or Agent Provocateur under power suits suggested a confident Western womanhood, silver-fringed Charleston bra-and-thong sets, purchased by Arab women for themselves, their daughters and daughters-in-law, displayed a similar assurance coupled with imaginative attitudes towards sexuality and desire. Interestingly, in both cotton and racy lingerie firms, Syrian women designers were practically non-existent. When they finally enter into the cut and thrust of manufacturing and create their own undergarments, they will not have to rely on business visionaries like Hanin's Moussalli to tell them how fast-paced their lives should be. For between children, home and, for many, work, few Syrian mothers, wives and sisters have a scant moment to themselves.

Textiles have formed part of the warp and weft of Aleppo society since the third millennium BC, as archaeological and documentary evidence clearly attests. Yet in the move away from workaday fabrics or traditional styles, a microcosm of broader and more profound patterns emerge. Namely, the irrepressible ingenuity of Syrian creativeness, continuing well into the twenty-first century; and the truth that Syria remains irrevocably integrated into the global trade network—notwithstanding attempts by Syrian rulers or US presidents to the contrary. It is the very popularity of the lingerie, both cotton and racy, and its far-reaching distribution which demonstrates how adept Syrians have been at negotiating a spectacular array of problems thrown at them from within and beyond their borders.

Many of Aleppo's factories have been destroyed since 2011, bombarded by the regime and looted by hungry Free Army militias. The *suqs* and medina have been hard hit by Assad's shelling; some have been destroyed. The city's economy has collapsed; its residential areas are barrel-bombed hells. It remains to be seen how Aleppo will recover from this latest and most massive crisis.

THE LOST CHILD IN OVERSIZED SHOES

Afra Jalabi

Wars are crowded with male faces, weapons and gruesome images. We know there are other things happening but we are struck anew when we are there on the ground to see for ourselves. In late January 2014, I had the chance to go inside Syria when a group of friends decided to visit liberated areas and deliver baby milk, winter clothes and some aid for local initiatives. More than 60 per cent of Syria is no longer under regime control, and these islands of vulnerable freedom are now called the liberated areas. What struck me first was the huge number of families, children and elderly people we encountered everywhere. Their faces are usually absent from war reporting. But their suffering is the reality of any conflict.

The first Syrians we came across at the edge of a small town north of Aleppo were two small children. The expressions on their faces hit us like bullets. Young faces but with ancient, sorrowful eyes. There, as the sun was setting, they were cycling around rubble and shelled buildings. What we didn't realise then was that we were going to see the same vacant, distant expressions on the face of every child. I was always relieved when some kid during our journey broke into tears at the mention of a killed parent, sibling or relative. The tears would soften the faces of these already aged children.

We were able to go further south into the country all the way to the famous Kafranbel, located south of Aleppo and north of Hamah, a town known for its civic activism, creative signs and large posters. We met many of the local artists and activists. But the faces of the children haunted me everywhere. Their eyes followed me even after we had left a place. In one small town, we were able to attend an exhibition of children's art that was held inside a cave to avoid the danger of sudden air raids. But it wasn't necessarily protected from an explosive barrel that could penetrate the earth into the belly of the cave. One of the drawings depicted a little bear with its heart cut up, the wool filling showing, and an eye falling out. There were drawings of body parts strewn around houses. One six-year-old girl had drawn rifles, Scud missiles, MiG-26 fighter jets and other weapons. The picture revealed a child whose innocence had been stolen by detailed military expertise.

It seemed people were walking normally everywhere in all the towns we passed, or sitting in front of their porches, but mostly in sombre silence. The houses we visited were so orderly, with spotless kitchens—perhaps the women's attempt to maintain sanity and order in a world that had gone chaotically insane. I had missed all this. Sometimes I had to stand still and become aware of the pine-scented air and the scene of the surrounding hills. I had not been to Syria for the previous six years.

Since being liberated by the Free Syrian Army in July 2012, this region of southern Idlib province had been targeted by regime air raids, mortar shells and even Scuds. The possibility of a regime air raid was present at every moment. On the ground, war suddenly looked different. It no longer had the face of males bearing weapons. It had the faces of children and the elderly, of clean kitchens, and shelters in caves.

We were surrounded by civilians of all ages, students, engineers, shopkeepers, farmers, mothers, doctors, and teachers. Some had become volunteers in the Free Syrian Army or were running the local councils and coordinating humanitarian and civic work. Women were elected to some of these councils. Danger was mixed up with hope, our aspirations for a new Syria. The ground had been liberated but the skies remained colonised by Assad's forces which could suddenly send down a chunk of hell indiscriminately on any area.

Meanwhile the liberated areas were becoming more vulnerable to an influx of foreign fighters who aimed to fill the power vacuum and, having more funds and being better armed, were prepared for efficient action. One young man, holding the hand of his fiancée, her hair covered in a tangerine-coloured scarf, said between clenched teeth, 'I don't want these people to rule over my mother, my fiancée or sisters.' He was referring to the newly arrived extremist forms of Islam, and his anxiety concerned the female members of his family becoming subject to a fanatical interpretation of Islam that seemed entirely foreign to local Syrians, who viewed themselves as already sufficiently religious. And we were in the north, one of the most conservative areas in Syria.

Having had similar concerns ourselves before crossing the borders, my (Christian) Syrian friend Hind Kabawat and I both decided to cover our hair. One of the Free Syrian Army liaison officers travelling with us insisted that we enter Syria as we were. 'I want you to know that among Syrians nothing has changed and you are still accepted the way you are. And I want you to see this for yourselves,' he said. 'If you cover your heads you'll never find out how welcome you'd be in any shape. The fact that you are here and that you care is what matters to these people.' Sadly things have shifted dramatically in recent months, often for the worse – although since January 2014 the most extreme Islamist militia of all – the Islamic State of Iraq and Syria (ISIS) – has been fought across the north by Islamist and secular militias and driven from many of its former strongholds.

Walking on the streets of Kensafra, a small town near Idlib, with a young mother, I kept asking what it felt like to live in such conditions. She started by counting the names of people who'd been killed in recent shelling. 'You're lucky today,' she added as we walked the streets of the little town. 'It's cloudy today and the fighter planes are not equipped to strike through cloud. They do it mostly on sunny days.' She then said softly, almost inaudibly, 'Every night we go to bed not knowing if we'll ever wake up again.' Two days after we left, Kensafra was hit and three people were killed.

Just before preparing to depart, and while my friends were waiting at an agreed meeting point, the young mother wanted me to meet one of her close friends who insisted on serving me my last cup of coffee in the town. She was the wife of a fallen hero killed by regime forces, and she lived with her sister-in-law, who also had lost her husband, the two are raising their children together. Her story distracted me from the coffee that was beautifully presented with a clear glass of cool water, in keeping with true Syrian etiquette, despite the modesty and simplicity of the house. She talked about the horrors of living at the mercy of the Syrian security forces who barged into towns and homes alike before the area was liberated. 'Once I saw a huge crowd in front of our house,' she said, 'and when I peeked from the window, I saw my fourteen-year-old son surrounded by the *mukhabarat'*, the regime's infamous secret agents.

The woman had rushed outside and broken through and grabbed her son's hand so she stood facing the agents. 'Move away, woman!' one of them screamed into my face, but I was determined to stand still and kept staring into his eyes. Juhaida explained that she and her son were trembling, but only within. 'I could feel the strongly beating pulse of his little wrist in my hand,' she said. 'He felt like a frightened little bird in my hand, but externally we both appeared to be calm.' One of the agents moved in closer and brought his rifle up right in her face, 'and placed the opening here, right on my neck,' she said, putting her finger on the spot. He told her, 'If you don't move away, you know what will happen in this instant.' Juhaida paused her narration for a few moments, then looked at me and said, 'I was willing to die. There was no way I could have let them take my son after they killed my husband.'

In the end her stillness and defiance made the other agents uneasy and they pressured their colleague to back off. 'You're a strong woman,' he told her, the rifle still pointed at her neck. 'I'm not,' Juhaida answered him. 'It's from God,' she then said softly. 'Then they finally backed off.'

I sat speechless and held my head in my hands, overcome by the story, being the mother of a fourteen-year-old boy myself. Finally I stood up and kissed her head, and told her, 'I only read about your kind in books; I've never met one in person.' We had to leave, just after I'd met my personal hero. But the problem is that they're everywhere. Heroes and heroines fill towns and streets. It's just that their stories are not being heard. We left Syria, leaving all of our new friends in the zone of insanity while we drove across the Turkish border to safety.

But the children kept on haunting me, including that boy whose courageous mother offered him another chance in the jungle of Assad's Syria.

The children continued to haunt me even after my return to Canada. One image still holds me captive, not so much because it's more gruesome than those that have come out of Syria lately, of gassed children and skeletal babies, but perhaps because it is by far the most painful. It's one of those that can haunt one's conscience perpetually, not only because its details speak volumes of misery and challenge us to the very core of our being, but also because it serves as a metaphor for an entire nation. It encapsulated forty-three years of abuse and horror under Assad, as well as the betrayal of the international community.

It's the image of a murdered child, killed most probably by a sniper, his body lying lifeless and beginning to decay. With a closer look one sees his oversized shoes and his oversized shirt and big bag. I became obsessed with this photo. I kept asking around and finally came across a piece on the Daraya Council page that provided some information. His name was Salim Zakour and he had been orphaned after losing his family and close relatives to shelling in the countryside. He was roaming the streets of Aleppo until a sniper took away his last hold on life.

The suffering of ordinary people forms the core of any conflict, and yet it is most often absent from media narratives. Perhaps it's absent because if it took centre stage we could not afford to look away as most of the world has done. Many observers and commentators on Syria draw parallels with Bosnia and Rwanda. But the one that almost never comes up, and which has many more commonalities with Syria, is the Spanish civil war, where legitimate demands for democracy and justice turned into a civil war involving many young fighters. And just as Nazi Germany and Fascist Italy supported Franco, Assad is now being supported by Russia and Iran, with weapons and even a key presence on the ground. In Spain, the world watched Franco crush a revolution and keep his grip on power for the next thirty-seven years.

But the world paid a hefty price. Appeasement of fascism in Spain and elsewhere in Europe eventually led to World War II, which killed over 60 million people and displaced many millions more, levelling many European capitals. Allowing Syria to implode is the current international approach, but Syria is becoming a black hole, and black holes exert an irresistible pull, sucking all those around into their depths of darkness. Syria is being systematically destroyed as the international community celebrates the (so far illusory) removal of Assad's chemical weapons, and the regime continues its brutal killing and crushing of Syrians by other means. Meanwhile the international 'peace movement' celebrates the stopping of American strikes without wanting to acknowledge that the real strikes on the Syrian people have not stopped for the last two and a half years.

What makes the media version of Syria deeply problematic is the language and context in which it is presented. At the moment the conflict is being posed as one between al-Assad and al-Qaeda. This reductionist equation erases the millions of Syrians who started a revolution to end tyranny. Their voices are missing. Their stories and sufferings go unheard. There are many reasons for this, one being the internationalisation of the conflict and the power games of the regional and international powers. But Islamophobia and Orientalist obsessions obfuscate many basic facts about Syria. Even respected journalists jump right into cheap tabloid-style sensationalism. When titles such as 'Syria's Descent into Holy War' are used by established journalists such as Patrick Cockburn, when Robert Fisk declares a strike against Assad is a strike for al-Qaeda (ignoring the fact that al-Qaeda's affiliates in Syria were vehemently opposed to American action), we know we have a strong case of Orientalism revisited. And when obsession with 'sex jihad' reaches fever pitch in the international media only for it to be revealed that no such thing ever existed, we know we are dealing with dated and lunatic obsessions about an Orient populated exclusively by fighters clad in exotic robes who decapitate their enemies before retiring to their harems. The way Syria has been covered is worth many studies: the deliberate omissions, the obsessive focus on irrelevant details, the exaggeration of certain barbarisms while other, larger ones are taken for granted, the specific recurrent tropes which indicate a deeply flawed relationship with the Arab world and an ignorance of the real and serious challenges faced by ordinary people throughout the region, their basic human rights and dignity as citizens of this world.

Syrians started their revolution as part of the uprisings sweeping the region with demands for *hurriah wa karramah* (freedom and dignity); specifically with demands for political reform and the release of prisoners of conscience. They demonstrated peacefully and organised local coordinating committees and community councils, only to be met by bullets, shelling and tanks besieging cities and towns. For the next six months Syrians endured the crushing weight of the regime by organising massive demonstrations and trying to create and strengthen local networks to make up for a forty-three-year hiatus in political and civic life. The regime, telling the outside world it was fighting against terrorists, hunted down, detained and uprooted the country's civil rights activists, especially those committed to nonviolence.

Tens of thousands of civil activists are currently languishing in horrific conditions in Assad's prisons (and perhaps being murdered – the United Nations provided proof in early 2014 of at least 11,000 killings of detainees in just one part of Assad's prison system). A Human Rights Watch report mentions Yahya Shurbaji and Ghayath Matar from Daraya, and Anas Shughry from Banyas, names which resonate with the Syrian public, and which didn't spring out of a vacuum. Yahya and his friend Ghayath, who was deeply influenced by Yahya's commitment to nonviolent principles of change, didn't suddenly appear handing out roses and sweets to security and army personnel. There had been a grassroots movement in Daraya for the previous fifteen years which pushed at the limits by engaging in positive civic activism. The activists organised neighbourhood cleaning campaigns, anti-smoking awareness drives, study groups, and the opening up of small book sharing libraries in private homes. Most were arrested back in May 2003. Yahya and his friends were sentenced to terms ranging from several months to four years for violating martial law by organising and congregating in groups, and for 'undermining the dignity of the nation.'

There were many attempts to push for a small margin to enable democratic reform in Syria before the revolution. The Damascus Declaration was formed in 2005 as an umbrella group to create an indigenous political alliance to push for gradual change. The signatories focused on a commitment to non-violent reform and the rejection of external help or intervention. Most of the initial 200 signatories inside Syria were imprisoned, and those of us in the diaspora who signed it found ourselves on Syrian security lists, unable to visit the country again. This was why my first visit in years was only possible in the areas freed from the regime.

There were many chances for this regime to spare the country and itself. Even when the revolution began, it could have responded differently. However, the regime stuck blindly to its military tactics and heinous security paradigm, and delivered the country to Iran and Russia to help it crush and kill the uprising. Having come to power through a military coup in 1970, the regime never had the true consent of the population, and hence it always viewed the Syrian people as potential enemies. Syrians discovered this during the revolution when they realised that the entire country was littered with tiny military airports ready to launch air-raids on their own towns and villages.

The nonviolent struggle in Syria was yet another attempt to create an opening for change and reform without annihilation and destruction. In one of the last posts of Ghayath Matar, a couple of days before his arrest on 6 September 2011, he wrote on his Facebook page: 'the reason we commit to nonviolence is not due to weakness or cowardice but because we believe in it as a moral principle and because we don't want to arrive at victory having destroyed our country.' That voice of sanity echoes now over the scorched landscape of Syria, where some cities like Deir ez-Zor or Homs have been completely destroyed. That voice is still there, although it is growing ever more faint. In a recent visit to one of the nonviolent activists by his relatives, Islam Dabbas spoke with his family in metaphors while agents monitored the conversation. He asked them, 'Why did our rose garden burn down?'

Nonetheless it is also a country where the *shabbiha* (pro-Assad thugs and militias) graffiti the walls with the threat 'Assad or we burn the country.' Ghayath Mater's tortured body, that body which had won the national silver medal for body-building, was returned dead to his family four days after his arrest. His two brothers have also been arrested and remain in prison. The nineteen-year-old brother of Anas Shugry, Salah, was detained at a check point in 2013 and is still a prisoner, incommunicado. These are only some Syrian stories.

Was the Syrian revolution too naïve, too young, to stand up to one of the most brutal tyrannies in modern history? Were the Syrians that young kid on the block trying to walk into oversized adult shoes with aspirations for freedom, in a world where the blood of children and civilians is worthless?

The blood of over 150 thousand killed testifies to this innocence and naïveté. But this very blood also testifies to the cruelty of today's international world order and the dated ethos of the UN Security Council. What is the value of anything we do, say, or invent in a world in which we move ships and war planes across oceans to secure oil reserves but don't bother blinking over eleven thousand children killed and an entire nation bleeding daily for over three years?

FROM HAMA TO DARAYA

Amal Hanano

1982

There is a woman who lives alone in Hama, Syria. She has been in mourning for thirty-two years, tormented by memories of her survival. One night in February 1982, when she was a young woman in her twenties, military forces raided the basement where she and the women in her family had been hiding, huddled with their neighbours. They had thought they were safe, sheltered from the mass murders and arrests that had become everyday occurrences in the historically quiet and conservative city.

On 2 February, President Hafez al-Assad's forces sealed Hama with tanks, effectively placing Syria's fourth largest city — with a population of 800,000 people at the time — under siege. With no communications to the outside world, Hama's men, women, and children lived alone in their terror— their cries unheard, their images unseen. By the end of that month, an estimated 20,000–40,000 people were killed. The exact number of dead will never be known. The mass graves will never be discovered. Countless others disappeared into Assad's prisons to be tortured for years, even decades. These men were left to rot to death and forgotten forever.

That night in the basement, screams mixed with the explosions from the soldiers' machine guns. The rain of bullets turned the screams into desperate final gasps. And then, silence. Within minutes, the young lady's family and friends had become a pile of corpses burying her underneath. It was her fate and her luck to have been covered by their bodies. She stifled her sobs, fought against the urge to vomit, and forced her own body to be as still as the heavy corpses.

While she pretended to be dead, she watched between the gaps of clothes and limbs as soldiers hacked off the women's's' hands to slip the valuable stacks of gold bangles off their wrists. She watched while the soldiers made crude jokes, mocking the dead. She waited until the room was as silent as the death that surrounded her. Only then did she allow herself to scream, but no sound came out of her mouth. She untangled herself from the pile of mutilated bodies that used to be her family and friends. She waited, terrified, for four days, before she walked out of the basement, covered in their dried blood. She was alive and alone.

Over the years, every now and then, she would decide to write her family's story and preserve the details so she would not forget. So when the time came to tell the story of Hama, everyone would know the truth of what happened to her family. She would sit and write. Every time she finished a draft, terror would consume her once more because she feared the incriminating pages. Everyone around her could potentially be a government informant. In Syria, as they say, even the walls have ears.

She would take the small stack of carefully penned pages—her memory's record—and burn them one by one in her stovepipe heater. A few years later, courage would creep back and she would attempt to write once more, vowing this time to save the pages. Every time she broke her promise to break her silence, even though that silence had merely been breached in the lonely space between herself and the page.

The process of writing and burning, remembering and repressing, speaking then falling silent, is the story of Syria under the rule of the Assad dynasty. We learned from a young age how to swallow our stories and bury our memories within us, as quickly as we learned to chant declarations of love by force, for a leader we did not love. Truth duelled with fear for four decades—and fear always won. Until 2011.

In the spring of 2011, the once impenetrable dam of repression began to crack and we were flooded with memories we never thought we would speak of in private, let alone discuss in public. For the first time, the Syrian people spoke without swallowing the words and wrote without burning the pages.

When I lived in Syria in the late eighties and nineties, fear was our mode of survival. Although no one discussed 'the events' of Hama, as they are called, I fantasised about recording the stories of the city's people. Of course, this fantasy remained in the realm of my imagination. Fear always trumped dreams in Syria till the uprising.

I never imagined I would begin to write about Syria in the midst of a series of revolutions across the Arab world, while witnessing dictators fall like dominos and the mightiest of regimes rattled to their core by the furious uprisings of the people. I never imagined watching the events of Egypt, Libya, Yemen, and Bahrain unfold in waves of undulating dreams and nightmares. I never imagined I would watch fearless Syrians chant for the downfall of Bashaar al-Assad while facing the same bullets and tanks that had killed thousands only twenty-nine years before. I never imagined I would write the truth while the regime was still in power.

What did I imagine? What we all used to imagine and say to ourselves— after every injustice and humiliation we witnessed or suffered—that the tyrants wouldn't last forever. That one day they would be gone. Then we would be free to finally release all our secrets, the ones the regime taught us to hide deep within ourselves.

But what we never talked about was how exactly this regime would cease to exist. We never got past the self-soothing utterance: 'He will not be able to rule us forever.' Imagining scenarios of a Syria without Assad—first the father and later the son—was enough. Enough to test our moral compasses and know beyond doubt that they had not corroded beyond repair. Enough to claim resistance, even though that resistance was confined to our limited imaginations. But we never went beyond fleeting thoughts.

In spite of our young nation's history of colonialism, our series of post-colonial military coups, and our four decades of dictatorship, in spite of the dark chapters of a raging civil war to our east and the still-messy aftermath of civil war to our west, in spite of being trapped within the clutches of an entrenched regime that planned to rule forever, we still believed somehow, sometime, there would be a Syria after Assad. We allowed ourselves these indulgent dreams of the pristine, liberated 'after', but not of the bloody, almost impossible, nightmarish 'during.'

After—that's when I planned to write the truth about living in Syria under Assad and how it felt to live in fear. But as we have always known, the only way to arrive at 'after' is by walking (and sometimes crawling) along a long road paved with the heavy sacrifice of our people's blood and tears.

None of us imagined that the road would be this bloody, or that the sacrifice would be this heavy.

For as long as I can remember, whenever we summoned the courage to speak, we whispered. We whispered behind closed doors, with the windows shut and shuttered, only in the company of closest family, with grandfathers darting their frightened looks into the dark corners of the room. They could never shake off the nagging feeling that someone was listening in the shadows. In Syria, there is always someone listening. If the whispers rose into an audible sound, or worse, formed unanswerable questions, the elders would immediately end all conversation. In those moments of self-enforced silence, the shadows in the corners of our living rooms seemed to grow darker and deeper, into black holes that threatened to swallow us whole.

Hama, an ancient city, was the symbol of this enforced silence. Hama, the site of a massacre, represented the evil that diminished an entire city into a painful example for the rest of the country, a reminder of what happens when the silenced dare to speak. Hama, the city of scars, was supposed to make us forget our voices. And it did. For twenty-nine years.

Of all the un-crossable taboos that existed in Syria, speaking about Hama was a red line no one dared cross. Hama was the landscape of blood and secrets. For my generation, Hama was experienced through secondhand accounts, overheard snippets of conversations between adults. We did not know exactly what had happened, how it happened, we just knew there once was a city and now only a depressing shell of that city existed. What really happened to Hama was a mystery. All we knew was that thousands had died that February of 1982 and that the events of Hama were the roots of our country's fear.

I imagined visiting Hama, knocking on doors, asking for stories, photographs, accounts, anything that would expose this hidden past. I wanted to hold in my hands tangible proof of these crimes no one spoke of except in whispers. Of course that never happened. It was never the right time to write or even speak about Hama.

But in March 2011, as we watched the birthplace of the revolution, the southern city of Dara'a, bleed, we remembered Hama. Even those who were not old enough to remember were taught the lesson of Hama. After decades of silence, the details of 'the events,' once buried deep in spaces we did not know were part of our anatomy, re-emerged clear and sharp, as if they had just happened yesterday.

As we watched the blood-stained news from Dara'a, the people of Hama began to speak in normal voices, not whispers, about what they had seen. Children murdered in front of their mothers and husbands shot execution style in front of their families. Bodies were left in alleys to rot overnight, until the military trucks rambled down the ravaged streets at dawn. The survivors, crouched behind the thick stone walls, listened to the menacing rumble and the thuds of their loved ones bodies as they were thrown into the back of the trucks into a towering heap. The blood flowed out of the back of the trucks, forming a stream that stained the ancient cobblestoned streets of Hama a crimson red. The screams of wives, daughters, mothers, were stifled by others in the house as they hid in closets and underground shelters. The secrets and details, once so masterfully concealed, came out with unstoppable force now.

It was as if Syrians had a primal need to utter the truth to anyone who would listen, as if they could not contain the memories any longer, as if they needed to scrub out the insides of their hearts, as if by finally releasing the stories, they would somehow be freed of the guilt of silence.

So we watched the events of March 2011 while in our hearts we were watching the events of February 1982. The YouTube videos projected the present but they also replayed the past. Finally we had the evidence, the images of what we had never seen but only imagined. Though it happened in another time, in another city, at the hands of the son instead of the father, we watched and remembered. We were split in half, dealing with our past by watching our present. We watched knowing very well what it means for a Syrian city to be sealed, knowing very well that what was happening in Dara'a—and what would happen over the next years in cities across Syria—had already happened before. Only this time we were not silent.

Syria's voice became fainter and fainter under Hafez al-Assad's rule until it disappeared completely after the massacre of Hama. The Syrian people's stories died with their voices. But Dara'a elevated the whispers into defiant chants.

When some have decided that having a voice is a crime worth killing for, and others have decided having a voice is a cause worth dying for, we knew we all must break our silence. It was time to bury fear. It was time to write the stories without burning the pages.

2012

There is a man in the Damascus suburb of Daraya. His name is Ziad. On the morning of 25 August 25, 2012, he was pulled out of his home by the regime's security forces along with the rest of the men in his family and led into the street. He was lined up with dozens of men who lived in the neighbouring buildings. One of those men was Anas Dabbas. I met Anas in early 2014 at a university in Chicago where he was invited to tell his story.

Daraya was the heart of the revolution's non-violent resistance. It is home to iconic revolutionary heroes such as Ghiath Matar and Yahya Sharbaji. Men who gave flowers and water to Bashar al-Assad's soldiers who shot unarmed protesters. Men who believed the path to freedom was by peaceful struggle. In the first months of the revolution, hundreds of protesters from Daraya were arrested. Matar, the beloved young leader, was tortured to death and his best friend Sharbaji has been detained since 2011. We don't know if he is dead or alive.

In the face of the brutality, locals formed Free Syrian Army (FSA) units to protect Daraya from the Syrian army's ruthless assaults. For a few brief months in 2012, the town was finally liberated from Assad forces. However, during that week in August, regime forces finally broke through the under armed FSA checkpoints and entered the city in tanks.

That morning, standing in the long row, Anas feared they would be rounded up and taken to prison like so many of his friends before him. Soldiers passed by each man asking random questions. Where are you from? Show me your ID card! Do you support the president? Anas remembers each interrogation being less than thirty seconds long. He says, 'what I didn't know is that those thirty seconds were our trial. And the sentence was death.' Anas was among the ones let free. He went back to his home. It had been looted and ransacked in front of the family's women. His family was upset and complained about their bad luck, until they heard endless rounds of gunshots outside.

They waited, terrified, until the streets were quiet once more. Hours later, Anas went outside and saw his neighbour Ziad, stunned speechless and covered in blood. Ziad pointed to the building next door. Anas walked inside and down the steps into the basement. The corpses of the men who had stood shoulder to shoulder next to him were piled on the ground. Over fifty bodies in total, including Ziad's two brothers. Ziad was supposed to be one of the murdered. Instead his fate was to be shielded by the men who were shot before him. As the corpses buried him, he instinctively did what the woman in Hama had done thirty years before – he pretended to be dead until the security forces left. When deathly quiet returned, he untangled himself from the bodies of the men who used to be his neighbours. He was alive and alone.

Ziad pointed towards the stairs. Anas went up to Ziad's apartment. Inside, they would find Ziad's wife and children, his brothers' wives and children, his mother, twelve people in total, all dead. Ziad broke his silence then. Ziad began to scream.

Anas took Ziad into his home, 'How could we leave him alone?' Anas tells his story in a a voice barely louder than a whisper. He tells me about the mosque down the street where they found over 100 bodies later that day. He tells me about his brother's family that was killed one week before the chemical weapons attack exactly a year later. His brother's family was killed by a shell that destroyed their home while they were inside. He tells me he is lucky to be alive. And I wonder how much of this gentle-spoken man is actually still intact.

He asks the American audience listening to his grave testimony, 'Why do you watch us and do nothing? Why is our blood so cheap?'

The story of a nation begins and ends with the stories of its people. For over forty years, the authoritarian regime had tried to make the story of Syria, and thus its destiny, the narrative of one person and of one family. When Syrians stood up to face the tyrant, his image shattered into a million pieces that reflected the multiplicity of the people. I always knew we lived within the confined walls of Assadism, but I did not realise that we had become ghostlike shells of ourselves. You never know how much of yourself has disappeared until you face a mirror of truth to expose what had been hidden behind the facade of false (and forced) loyalties.

Growing up in Syria, silence and fear dictated every facet of daily life. You are taught to be suspicious of everyone and everything. You are taught to glue your gaze to the ground when walking on the street.

When I visited Aleppo in the summer of 2011, at the beginning of the revolution, I had no idea what I would see, what I would write, or even if I would write anything at all. I wondered whether this 'project' I had in mind would evaporate like my project for Hama from many years before. I feared my resolve would fade and that I would swallow my words like the woman from Hama. But I didn't.

I wrote from Aleppo and continued after I returned to America. I wrote throughout the revolution, in all its phases, forging relationships with people I had never met before. Some of these people are now dead. I never imagined that I would meet men who would become my brothers on Skype and later would watch them die on YouTube, over and over. I never imagined that while unearthing the stories of Hama, the stories of our past, I would be told stories of its repetition in the present. Stories of our future.

The months and years passed, and the number of dead rose dramatically as the revolution morphed from a peaceful resistance into an armed struggle. Our enemies multiplied and the line between friend and foe blurred beyond recognition. The revolution changed and we changed with it. As we enter its fourth year, it's difficult to separate what we still hold from our former selves from that which has been lost forever. Hope died with each setback and was resurrected with each small victory, over and over.

As the cliche goes, history repeats itself. In Syria, massacres repeat themselves. This cycle of violence perpetrated on the same people by the same family, generation after generation of both people and dictator, will one day stop. People, weak people, will ask: Was it worth it? This question will be worthless to Syrians. All that will matter is that one day we will have fought our way to the other side of the question. The answer is always the same, in 1982, 2011, 2014: there is no price for freedom.

There is a direct link on our path of history from Hama to Dara'a, from 1982 to 2011, from the heart of Syria to its southern border; a path we had ignored. The journey from Hama to Dara'a — across history and memory

— is the journey of our nation moving from the end of darkness to the light, it is the journey from blind acceptance to defiant resilience. It is the Syrian Awakening; as if, as a nation, we realised that there would never be an after without a during, without facing the known and the unknown in all of its terror.

This journey that had taken decades was as clear as the writing on the school walls by the Dara'a teenagers who did not know they would spark a revolution, but knew they wrote the truth. With their words, 'the people want to topple the regime,' they wrote of our collective desires and echoed our decades-old dreams.

They wrote to awaken the rest of us, to face our tyrants but also to face the red trace that had led from Hama to Dara'a. Their words became a river that overflowed across the land, connecting everything that happened before to everything that would unfold after, until the map of Syria became a sea of our people's blood.

We awakened not only to fight the oppression and brutality that had defined us, but to discover who we were. I discovered my story was not confined to my personal history but intertwined in the stories of the people I would meet across Syria and the friendships I would build in time of revolution. After years of imagining myself as a future storyteller of the past, I found myself absorbing the epic landscape of blood and heroism that was our present. And so one day I wrote the story of the woman in Hama. A story that will now never be burned about a family that will now never be forgotten.

The road from Hama to Dara'a illuminated what we had always known: there was nothing more criminal than our silence; nothing more powerful than our voices; no price too high to claim 'the after' with our own hands; and most of all there was never a better time to write the painful pages of our past without swallowing the words and no better time to release our secrets without burying the evidence.

There is no better time to tell the truth than right now. What I didn't realise is how difficult it would be to tell the truth. And to find it, you must go back.

Back to the stories of the past, the ones that led to the revolution. And now we go back to the stories of the revolution. The ones that have become epic reminders of what happens when it all goes wrong. When, in moments of weakness, you question, was our parents' silence better, smarter, stronger than our brothers' and sisters' chants? When you ask, were we really paying the price of silence, or did silence protect us then from the hell unleashed in Syria today? When doubt contaminates your beliefs, you go back to the woman in Hama who still burns her story. And you go back to Anas, who bravely tells his story over and over, so everyone is forced to listen and never forget.

In spite of it all, you continuously choose hope over fear, choose not to be buried by grief, choose to survive.

That is the only choice. If I had the chance again, I would choose to be like Anas. I would choose not to swallow the stories. Even if it means to write them over and over, with different names and different dates, I would write the same story with the same bloody ending. I will live on in this maddening repetition with my people until the cycle ends. Until we can finally close the chapter and call this nightmare we lived through a cold and distant history.

But something else happens when you tell a story. After you narrate it, the tale is transferred to the reader. These Syrian stories now belong to you: Anas's; Ziad's; the woman from Hama's; Dara'a's story; and mine. You are free to do with them as you wish. You can choose to forget that you even read these lines. Or you can choose to do something different. You can choose not to turn away.

In the time it took you to read these lines, more people have died in Syria. More stories, more voices, have been erased forever. When you realise what they died for, then choosing to tell their stories is not a choice at all.

NOT EVEN THE BASEMENT ESCAPES

Frederic Gijsel

Writing about Syria has become impossible without seeing things in the light of the revolution and the conflicts developing since March 2011. It's difficult to remember how things were just two years ago, right before the start of the uprising. For people who spent a long time there, and even for Syrians themselves, that reality has been absorbed by one more poignant. That time seems to matter little now that every Syrian has lost friends or family.

Nevertheless, I would like to step back for a moment in order to observe the Damascene cultural scene in February and March 2011, in the weeks ahead of the imprisonment of a dozen children in the southern city of Dara'a and the start of the uprising. That period now feels like a vague dream, a bubble which has suddenly burst.

Syria before the uprising was a place of ambiguity and paradox. The cultural sphere of the 2000s showed signs of opening up. The young Assad was given time and credit to steer the country towards a more open future, and for a short period, now known as the Damascus Spring, he did – at least superficially. After forty years of cultural stagnation the transition appeared huge. As government loosened its control over culture and media, private newspapers were established and a creative industry developed around Syrian *musalsalat* (TV serial dramas). New galleries were founded, like Mustafa Ali's in the former Jewish quarter, and every week new exhibitions showing talented young Syrians opened in Damascus, although all were still monitored for potential subversion. The Damascus Spring can hardly be considered a revolutionary period: the *mukhabarat* still lurked around every corner, and if one of the few bookstores dared to sell Khaled Khalifa's prize-winning novel *In Praise of Hatred*, its proprietor would have rapidly found himself in prison. The *glasnost* didn't last long either. After several months permits were withdrawn and the opening cultural space closed again. Any hope that the regime would make a voluntary transition towards an open society was lost.

Nevertheless, the situation didn't return entirely to the dark days. Damascus seemed to have found a new spirit and at times attained a tantalising energy; it had grown into a city where artists felt more at ease. Right before the uprising the Syrian art scene was still defined by the famous red lines drawn by regime censors, but on the fringes these were exciting times. Within the system of control there was space for ambiguity; and some artists attempted to play a major role in defining it. Syrians have a flawless intuition in pointing out the boundaries of the permitted and creating their niche straddling the lines, like someone putting a foot on the borderline and plainly challenging the gatekeepers: will you arrest me while I'm not crossing your line?

In February 2011 I arrived in Damascus to conduct research on a poetry club called Bayt al-Qasid, the House of Poetry, held every Monday in the basement of a downtown hotel. I was especially interested in the tension between the free speech of poetry and a regime obsessed with controlling the cultural sphere. Bayt al-Qasid, and the cultural scene in general, was the progeny of the schizophrenic marriage between freedom and control, and occupied a position between these parents.

It's Monday night, a quarter to ten. I go down the stairs of the Fardoss Hotel in downtown Damascus and enter the dimly-lit basement, which has no physical connection to the outside world and feels like a cave. At the bar men and women sip beer and arak while they take a puff of their cigarettes and chat with their neighbours. Through the thick smoke the contours of the basement can be perceived. On the left there are small tables which have reserved tagged on them and a red comfy couch seated with grey-haired men and women. In the far left corner stands a catheter with a microphone sticking out. On the walls hang black and white pictures of Mahatma Gandhi and Malcolm X, giving the impression that important issues will be addressed and big changes are expected. The place fills up quickly, tables are taken, the couches are filled, chairs go quickly. The central arena is filled with standing people and right in front of the catheter there's a group of mostly foreign students sitting on the floor. At ten the place is packed, filled with cigarette smoke, the smell of beer, the sound of laughter and busy talk.

Then a man in worn-out jeans and a leather jacket enters the room. He greets everyone, the waiters, the people at the bar, the ones in the reserved seats and the ones on the floor. In his hand he carries a beer and a cigarette. After having greeted every single person in the room he walks towards the catheter and takes the microphone. Welcome to Bayt al-Qasid!

Bayt al-Qasid, the House of Poetry, was one of the most unique happenings in Syria. From its arrival on the cultural stage in 2006 it grew into one of the best known poetry reading sessions in the country and likely the best attended. It was founded and organised by Lukman Derky, a well-known writer and public figure and grew from a closed invites-only reading into an event which attracted a crowd of around one hundred visitors each Monday. The way poetry was treated in the Bayt al-Qasid may have seemed disrespectful to those accustomed to listening to poetry in a reverent way. Poetry had to compete with heavy drinking, with the shouting of both the public and Lukman himself, and most importantly with utter chaos. Evenings were full of contrasts and surprises: classical poetry skilfully read by grey-haired men, the heckling when performers made mistakes in their grammar, the men gazing at the women, someone starting up a tune on the *oud*, the singing of Kurdish songs. Bayt al-Qasid was a place of pleasure and hedonism. People came for beer, for laughter, for seduction, or simply for a night out. According to Lukman, the classical poet occupies a position of authority, disconnected from the public. He put poetry back where it belongs: amongst the audience. Members of the crowd volunteered to perform so the performer would never be in a position of superiority; there was hardly any separation between the two. The attendants themselves were the poetry.

The venue was for all people to enjoy. It didn't matter whether they were educated in European universities or roamed the streets of a conservative Damascene suburb; the audience made a colourful collection of genders, ages, nationalities and ideologies. Some were well-established writers and artists, some students of literature, others were amateur poets living the bohemian life or simply people who came to drink away their sorrows. The diversity of Bayt al-Qasid was Lukman's explicit intention, and he claimed that 'We are open for the drunk and the bourgeois.'

During the Monday-night sessions the microphone was open to anyone who wanted to share poetry, without the approval of any official. Thus the literary range was enormous (as was the variation in quality), ranging from ancient pre-Islamic poetry to modern classics like Mahmoud Darwish and

Nizar Qabbani, to self-written poetry, both by struggling novices and practised literary poets.

If one only focuses on the political aspects of a place like Bayt al-Qasid one risks losing track of these poetic dimensions, but politics and poetry are very hard to separate.

When I asked Lukman how he defines good and bad poetry, he responded:

'Bad poetry doesn't exist. There is either poetry or no poetry.'

'So what is poetry?'

'Poetry enchants and has to be believed. If you can believe it, it has charmed you. It is the expression of the truth, not in long boring books but in a few powerful sentences.'

This is the point where politics came into play. The expression of truth inevitably raised the question of how to deal with the boundaries of free speech that the government had erected. The only way this space of freedom could exist in an authoritarian context was by limiting itself. The nearly anarchic nature of the basement could not have existed without the approval of the security apparatus. The space was granted, and if necessary could be closed at any given moment. In order to remain on the cultural scene, Bayt al-Qasid had to walk the thin line between transgression and compliance; it had to play the government's game. It was an illusion of openness within a framework of control. In Syria nothing was as it seemed.

So it would be incorrect to typify Bayt al-Qasid simplistically as a place of political resistance. In fact, the man behind Bayt al-Qasid, Lukman Derky, stressed that 'Bayt al-Qasid is not a political place. Our prime agreement is to keep it as a poetic place.' (He didn't mention who this agreement was with). 'People make fun of politics, so we have no political motives. There are great things being read and written about politics. Politics is part of the poetic range so there can also be political poetry in Bayt al-Qasid. People read about struggle, liberation, communist issues, poverty... Enough! There is space for freedom in Bayt al-Qasid; there's no censorship, no pre-reading, and the microphone is open to everyone. The only condition is to speak for a maximum of two minutes.'

The poetry nights are attended by *mukhabarat* agents. Everybody knows how to recognise them. A story recounted by one of the regulars shows that these agents were sometimes challenged, even becoming objects of mockery: 'I remember several years ago there was this crazy moment. Lukman recognised one of the *mukhabarat* quietly sipping his beer. Lukman said in the microphone that the guy should come to the front and read like everybody else. He said: you can read anything you want, even the report you're going to give to your boss tomorrow. We never saw that guy again'.

This was a playful deformation of the social order with the representative of authority being called to account. On moments like these one had the impression that the power roles had momentarily changed. Although this change couldn't manifest itself beyond the confinements of the basement, it did a good job in confusing the system. So Bayt al-Qasid functioned like a hall of mirrors. It wasn't exactly clear who was being fooled and who was doing the fooling.

The censorship is not necessarily executed in formal ways. After years of being confronted with nosy authorities, Syrians internalised the red lines. This meant that even without proper monitoring, people often performed self-censorship. Syrians knew very well how far they could go in criticising the government, but at the same time how vague and arbitrary those lines could be. Lukman's claim of the absence of censorship is thus very relative and rather cynical.

Yet Lukman's vision of Bayt al-Qasid is not necessarily anti-political. By trying to keep it a poetic place, politically neutral, Lukman created space for ambiguity, for contrasting sides of the social and political spectrum to come together. He was in charge of safeguarding this conceptual universe at times when things threatened to spin out of control. This meant that when performers threatened to cross the red lines set by the regime, Lukman intervened.

It brings to mind a term coined by the French philosopher Michel Foucault (1926–1984) shortly before his death. Heterotopia was first introduced in the article 'Of Other Spaces'. For Foucault, 'heterotopias are places of Otherness whose existence sets up unsettling juxtapositions of incommensurate objects which challenge the way we think, especially the way our thinking is ordered.' In these counter-sites a kind of enacted utopia can be found in which the real sites are simultaneously represented, contested and inverted. Foucault argues that heterotopias are spaces of illusion. They give the impression of freedom while they are just as much spaces of surveillance. Heterotopian spaces do not exist solely by themselves; they are related to the hierarchy that created their conditions of existence, to which they can perform alternatively. Heterotopia is related to Foucault's more general idea about power: there is no 'outside' of power. While there is always resistance to power, it is never external in relation to power.

Bayt al-Qasid is the ultimate heterotopian space: being a space of in-between, a space of illusion, of utopia and dystopia, and a combination of market, cafe, brothel, public arena, spectacle and place of theatrical entertainment. It symbolises the impossibility of being outside of power. The illusion of freedom that can be experienced in Bayt al-Qasid does not oppose the system of control, but rather confirms it.

Bayt al-Qasid's paradoxical relation to power wasn't exceptional; rather, it was typical for the ordering of power since the collapse of Bashaar al-Assad's early reform efforts. A few other artists had some space to test the limits of the regime, notably cartoonist Ali Ferzat, an interesting case since he's witnessed many constellations of power since he entered the cultural stage in the sixties, before the Ba'ath Party came to power. Bashaar al-Assad was said to be a fan of his work, and met Ferzat personally. In 2000, at the beginning of Bashaar's presidency, Ferzat was able to start a satirical magazine, *al-Domari*, in collaboration with Yasser al-Azma, an actor best-known from various *musalsalat* (soap operas) and an expert in mocking Arab societies and leaderships. But soon the red lines closed in again, and the magazine shut down in 2003. Still Ferzat was granted considerable space to criticise the government in covert, ambiguous ways. When the uprising began Ferzat spoke out explicitly against the violent reaction to the protests, and depicted the president on his way out hitching a ride with Gaddafi. This was his final fall from grace in the eyes of regime supporters: Ferzat was beaten up and had to flee the country.

Once artists left the safety of ambiguity and started expressing their opinions explicitly, the bubble of freedom burst. Some had more space to manoeuvre than others. Those who were under the radar of the international community were most at risk. During my time in Damascus I heard of a young female writer imprisoned for alluding to the regime in a still unpublished novel.

This is not to say that people like Lukman Derky or Ali Ferzat were toys of the regime. They worked on their own projects for which they had to carve out space throughout the years. Their prominent positions weren't granted to them but rather were the result of a long-term balancing act between artistic independence and compliance in order to keep on operating, thereby trying to enlarge the sphere of movement. Relations between the cultural actors of that time and the regime cannot be captured in a simplistic binary. Such a scheme would fail to capture the complexity and contradictions. The truth is more poetic than that.

On 15 March 2011 in the town of Dara'a in the southern Hauran region popular protests broke out after local children were arrested for writing anti-regime slogans on the wall of their school. The military intervened with heavy weapons, causing several deaths. A few simple words were enough to start a nationwide uprising.

21 March

Lukman was in a good mood when I entered the Fardoss Hotel. The basement was full, but many regulars were missing and there were more unknown visitors. But the basic geography of the place remained the same: lonely men and women at the bar, the Iraqis between the foreigners and the villagers. Samir the soft-natured bodybuilder who must be one of the few people who comes especially to listen to poetry, the grey-haired Abu Ahmed, Farouk and Shakespeare. The evening began with a reading of Dante by an Italian student. Then Albrus, who as usual tried to read in classical Arabic but made too many mistakes and was corrected and booed by the audience. Then Farouk came up with a reading of Nizar Qabbani, one of the greatest Syrian poets, which was received warmly by the public. Next two girls played an intimate duet on the cello and the guitar. The crowd was willing and generous; it was a good night for poetry. Shakespeare read an old, well-known poem from Ummayad times, in which the audience loudly participated. As usual the night disintegrated, people left and new ones entered, most notably Hassan the dandy, never too shy to seduce foreign girls once they were drunk. Because it was Newroz, the Kurdish New Year, Lukman started singing Kurdish songs, and the evening transformed into an anarchistic celebration, completely forgetting the world outside the basement.

The centre of the club was now taken by dancing men and women, dancing in groups, in pairs or individually. The evening reached towards ecstasy. In the ensuing wildness and confusion, Malcolm X fell off the wall and sat on the couch. Suddenly a young man approached the catheter as if he were to cheer up the crowd. Instead he took the microphone and shouted: 'Support the martyrs of Dara'a! Remember the martyrs of the

Hauran!' Then Lukman took the microphone away from him and told everyone to go home. Lukman left the building. The rest followed.

With that final shout Bayt al-Qasid was silenced. The play of ambiguity and illusion had to give way to a harsher game. It was the end of Bayt al-Qasid and the end of a period that will never return, for better or for worse.

PROTECTING THE CULTURAL HERITAGE

Ross Burns

The tragedy which has overwhelmed Syria during the past three years has few precedents in recent history in terms of its savage consequences for the civilian population. Leaving aside plague or epidemics on the scale of the influenza outbreak at the end of World War One, the loss of life and prolonged suffering among Syrian civilians is probably unprecedented for centuries, possibly since the last Mongol invasion under Tamerlane in 1400. The world has largely lost interest in a steadily rising death toll, which now probably exceeds 140,000. In a conflict involving human losses on such a scale, it may seem perverse to be distracted by what has happened to the country's rich store of monuments. But Syria's cultural heritage is invaluable, and its loss would leave us all diminished.

Before the conflict began, awareness of Syria's extraordinary collection of ancient and Islamic sites had barely begun to penetrate beyond scholarly circles. Syria's antiquities had been overshadowed by the European fascination with places linked to the Biblical narrative, often providing a distorted picture of the Middle East as a whole. The regions of the interior had been seen largely in the light of religious preoccupations that downplayed the significance of any events not directly convenient in terms of the Biblical narrative or which saw the Islamic experience largely in terms of Western preoccupations.

That picture had begun to change in recent decades. In a recent thoughtful editorial in the *Palestine Exploration Quarterly*, the Keeper of the Middle East Department at the British Museum, Jonathan Tubb, noted that the enlightened attitude of the Syrian Department of Antiquities and Museums in the 1960s and 1970s had paid off in terms of the opening up of a new perspective on Syria's role in Bronze and Iron Age. The Directorate-General of Antiquities and Museums (DGAM) invited the

Italian archaeologist Paola Matthiae to explore the major mound at Tell Mardikh south of Aleppo, one of a series of discoveries that filled many gaps in our appreciation of Bronze and Iron Age history and highlighted 'the outstanding contribution Syrian archaeology has made to our understanding of Old World civilisation'.

Northern Syria was once seen as virtually *terra nullius* — or a vacuum occupying a space between other powers. But after the Italian results began to be published, it emerged as a major centre of civilisation in itself. In Tubb's words: 'we are dealing with an urbane and sophisticated people who, far from being the recipients of an external culture were, in many instances, the initiators'. The Biblical accounts had overlooked a whole world at its doorstep but the new findings placed Syria 'at centre stage in the archaeological theatre'.

While Syria had been drawn only marginally into the treasure hunt of the great European institutions — unlike Iraq, it was not plundered for late nineteenth century European collections — it is only in recent decades that we have begun to appreciate fully its central role in many periods. Moreover, while only a few sites presented the same 'wow' effect as Karnak or the West Bank in Egypt, it had begun to be more widely appreciated in recent decades that Syria retained a much richer tapestry of surviving remains across the ages than any part of the ancient world. When I first lived in Syria in the mid 1980s, the number of tourist visitors was almost insignificant. By 2010 it had swollen to a seasonal flow that brought crowds of visitors each day to its most celebrated sites such as Palmyra, Aleppo, Bosra or Apamea. That still left hundreds of other sites only rarely exposed to visitors, providing the more intrepid tourist with a real sense of 'discovery'. What impressed visitors most, though, was the extraordinary openness of Syrians to outside visitors, who were welcomed with unstinting generosity.

Over the years, I was even more impressed by the fact that a growing proportion of visitors to sites were day-tripping Syrians. The country's education system had increasingly exposed them to the value of the past in instructing them about their own society. Syria was not the only nation to appreciate the value of past remains in framing the picture of a present society. Many other nations in the East Mediterranean area still heavily intervene to ensure that the past presents the 'right' message. Inconvenient phases are often downplayed or even airbrushed out of the tapestry. Faced with a pattern of cultures that was impossibly mixed, Syria adopted a relatively open-minded approach. It allowed in scores of foreign excavation teams each year including from countries whose governments took a hostile attitude to Syria's policies in the Middle East.

There was also the widespread structure of support that Syria deployed to ensure that the finds emerging from these researches were properly recorded and presented. While the record in terms of the spread of museums, storerooms and publication of research results could always be improved, it was making great progress in the years preceding the present crisis. Every province had at least two museums (split usually between archaeological remains and recreations of folk traditions), while specialist museums and the two major national collections in Aleppo and Damascus sought to give the broader picture of the nation's past.

Moreover, Syria also benefited from the lessons learnt in neighbouring societies that have experienced crises resulting in disastrous consequences for their national collections and for exposed archaeological sites and buildings. The media clamour over the 'sacking' of the Baghdad National Museum in 2003 had shown the potential weaknesses that museum and archaeological authorities had to guard against. The high priority that the Lebanese authorities had given after the end of the Lebanese Civil War in 1990 earlier underlined the importance of restoring symbols of national 'identity' such as the National Museum in Beirut. Contact through bodies such as UNESCO or ICOMOS (International Council on Monuments and Sites) had also brought a wider appreciation of measures which allowed for the protection of historic deposits—removal of smaller items to secure locations (such as the Banque du Liban in the case of Lebanon), moving other deposits to a wide variety of safe houses to prevent full-scale plundering, and shielding larger items with caissons, often in basement spaces. These measures are understandably not widely advertised, thus inevitably contributing to a sense—not always warranted—of historic remains being abandoned to their fate.

In the present crisis, Syria is considerably more exposed to events than either Iraq or the Lebanon, but it has the advantage of a relatively well-implanted supervisory and protective system. The events of the last three years have sorely tested this apparatus but it is worth bearing in mind that parts of the system still function and can provide a platform for recovering from the disaster that now overwhelms Syria's past.

So, what has been damaged? There is no clear answer to this question since no one has access to all parts of the country. The pattern of fighting often shifts unpredictably across the land area, making even impromptu checks impossible. Since the start of the fighting, I have kept a checklist of sites or buildings that have reportedly been subject to armed conflict, shelling or looting. At the moment my checklist of sites or major monuments said to have been damaged has just over 100 entries, including multiple entries for monuments within Aleppo and Homs, where fighting has spread across the historic urban centres.

The information assembled comes from two main sources: social media postings carefully brought together, in particular by the France-based website, the Association for the Protection of Syrian Archaeology (APSA); from reports issued by the Syrian Government's own Directorate-General of Antiquities and Museums (DGAM); and from material posted on UNESCO's website. The DGAM has participated in various UNESCO efforts to draw attention to the need to protect historical remains including through web-based courses and gatherings hosted outside Syria. International efforts to limit the scale of damage have also focussed on the prevention of illegal trafficking through Interpol. Three years into the present crisis, it is possible to say that the challenge of protecting cultural and historical remains has been well flagged and that the picture often conveyed in media accounts of a free-for-all involving widespread destruction is so far confined to a few cases.

However, this is not an argument for complacency. The picture could change at any time; massive amounts of artillery and aerial explosives are being deployed; the loss of the Aleppo Great Mosque minaret shows how itchy or simply nervous trigger fingers can bring disaster in a flash; the nature of the conflict changes by the month; and there is much we probably do not know at the moment - especially about areas now under the control of Islamic extremist groups with seriously iconoclastic agendas.

Doing nothing is not an option. The international community has an obligation to show it is serious about agreements which most nations (including Syria) have signed, including the 1954 Hague Convention for the Protection of Cultural Property in the Event of Armed Conflict and its subsequent Protocols. To let these issues pass unremarked would send a wrong signal and there is some evidence over the past three years that even at the popular level the preservation of cultural heritage is seen as important in Syria. Many posts by Syrians to social media sites repeat the point that archaeological remains are a part of Syria's identity and will be an important factor in the country's revival.

Are reports of destruction exaggerated? This question cannot be answered definitively until the conflict dies down and access is possible. Media coverage unfortunately lumps together reports of damage as if they are roughly equally extensive and significant. Many are unverified reports of damage to monuments, often clearly exaggerated since photos accompanying Facebook reports of 'destruction' reveal superficial or secondary damage that could readily be repaired. Given that much loose description has been involved, I have tried a more quantitative attempt to assess the level of damage. Of the 100 or so sites (a handful are probably buildings not of historical significance but included until this can be verified), I would assess the likely degree of damage according to the following four categories:

1. Seriously threatened involving structural damage — 6 sites or buildings (plus one site of unverified provenance)

2. Reparable with visible damage but not structurally threatened — 50

3. Removal of significant material (through looting, illegal digging, bulldozing) — 21

4. Minor or unverified damage — 25.

Of the six most damaged sites/buildings of major historic value, three are in the central area of Aleppo where the confrontation has been particularly savage (the Great Mosque's priceless Seljuk-era minaret is one of the few structures to have disappeared entirely) and where significant structural damage to two other central religious buildings has occurred. While Homs is the other urban centre that has been particularly badly damaged, it has been difficult to verify the full consequences of the shelling. Earlier pictorial coverage indicated destruction across the walled area but not necessarily sufficiently concentrated to bring down buildings.

Virtually half the sites examined are in the second group, though it needs to be added that the degree of damage in the not-structurally threatened category can vary from relatively minor or incidental to cosmetically significant deterioration. This pattern of secondary damage reflects cases where the ruthless targeting of civilian housing had been the prime objective and it needs to be emphasised that destruction in civilian housing areas is vastly more extensive.

Sites in category 3 (looting) are perhaps of the greatest long-term concern. If government authority has broken down in an area, there is little that can be done to bring order to a situation where neither lives nor normal means of protective intervention can be assured. Many communities are in deep distress in this crisis even if they have escaped the immediate effects of mass bombardment of civilian housing. For most, normal means of livelihood have long since gone. Societies that have survived on savings or through self-sustaining agriculture have subsequently found their resources coming to an end. Many have been forced to leave their homes and to camp in areas deemed more secure from clashes, existing on the margins of already-stressed communities. Even before the crisis, a large proportion of young people were without jobs or economic prospects. In these situations, and given the massive deprivation suffered by civilians who find themselves resorting to shelter in ancient tombs, houses or caves, it seems rather precious to highlight the risks to monuments.

While forgery of antiquities or pilfering through opportunistic finds have long been part of the Syrian scene, illegal traffic was in the past addressed through draconian laws. With the withdrawal of government services in many areas, a more blatant pattern of plundering, forgery and illicit trade has clearly flourished in numerous areas. In some cases, regime security forces themselves have taken the opportunity to search out and sell objects even resorting to heavy machinery for the task; in others the rebel forces have turned their hands to opportunistic digging and even bulldozing.

Until we have better information, the extent of illicit digging at sites (particularly ones remote from permanent settlement) cannot be clarified, but it is clear from satellite imagery that virtually the whole of the walled area of Roman Apamea in the Orontes Valley has been comprehensively pock-marked through two to five metre wide digs by treasure seekers. Twenty other sites are reported to have been plundered but the degree of success in finding 'treasure' could vary. It is, of course, questionable how much of marketable value is actually unearthed by such means. The point is rather that once material has been removed from its context (both location within a site and in terms of its stratigraphic position in time) the damage to the historical interpretation of finds is immense.

It is also noteworthy that almost 75 per cent of sites (categories 2 and 4) represent damage that could be readily repaired. One skill set that Syria hasretained was a body of experienced stonemasons. Most major cities require that inner city facades be built in stone (even modern projects). The DGAM has also gained invaluable experience in the use of modern engineering know-how to restore sites. Although the results have sometimes been criticised as insufficiently sensitive to the original, their methods have been considerably more correct than the procedures pursued in neighbouring countries, for instance Saddam Hussein's highly imaginative recreation of Babylon.

DGAM reconstruction projects in recent decades included the Great Mosque at Hama, which was almost entirely reduced to rubble in the 1982 clash between regime forces and the Muslim Brotherhood. As we have seen in other massive restoration projects—such as the rebuilding of over 100 mosques after the 1992 Cairo earthquake—there are risks in such large-scale projects that can bring new hazards through the use of rushed techniques or by applying modern materials and cement/plaster. To my knowledge, such problems have been largely avoided in Syria. In particular, recent restoration work in Syria by the Aga Khan Trust has built up a core of knowledge and technical experience whose results, ironically, were already evident through the extensive work on the restoration of the Aleppo Citadel (completed just before the 2011 crisis) and on the Ismaili castle at Masyaf on the western side of the Orontes Valley.

There are, though, a few damaged structures in Syria that will require rebuilding from the ground up. It is worth noting, for example, that even the delicate decorative friezes of the Seljuk minaret of the Aleppo Great Mosque owed much of their brilliant detail in their pre-2004 manifestation to restoration work done in the course of the twentieth century. The big challenges will be finding the funds and sufficient skilled workmen, but post-civil war Beirut has shown what results can be achieved with the right approach.

This is a conflict in which both sides have a patchy hold over the activities of their forces. Though the DGAM has not been inactive, it can do little in most areas to address the problems arising from the country's slide into widespread anarchy. Syrian official forces clearly treat many areas strewn with sites of historic significance with little regard for the remains beneath their tank tracks or in the way of their artillery. Yet it is also true to say that there are few signs of deliberate, targeted destruction of historic sites or even the selective shelling of Islamic structures. Some mosques in rebel-held territory (for example, in Dara'a, Homs and Aleppo) have been targeted presumably because their minarets were still the most prominent elevated points in the landscape and had been used by rebels as sniper or observation points. Cases of wilful destructive shelling of historical remains just to punish a community have been rare. A significant exception would appear to be the shelling of the upper structure of the extraordinary *nymphaeum* or public water fountain in classical Bosra. And unofficial Hizbullah propaganda videos have gloated over the destruction of the shrine of Khaled ibn al-Waleed, a companion of the Prophet revered by Sunnis, in Homs. Media coverage focussing on damage to monuments may lead us to believe that civilian casualties are 'collateral' damage and the monuments the targets. Tragically, the opposite is usually the case.

Perhaps as a result of the international coverage of the fate of its monuments, there is some evidence that on both sides — and certainly among civilians caught in the middle — there is an appreciation of the need to protect the country's heritage. The fact that APSA has been able to post so much material from local sources alerting us to the risk to monuments reflects the fact that even in the worst affected areas there are citizens aware of the issue's importance. In a few cases, through the efforts of locals, tombs, houses or churches of historic value have been protected. Realistically, however, there is a limit to how effective communities can be in fending off bulldozers or raiding parties.

The new factor in recent months, however, has been the rise of the Islamic State of Iraq and Syria (ISIS) in northern Syria. Largely outsiders, its cadres have no stake in the country's eventual recovery, but they do have an iconoclastic agenda. Their ideology involves hostility to all but the most sober expressions of Islamic belief, and their targets have included sites with Shi'ite or Sufi associations.

It took at least two generations for Damascus to recover from Tamerlane's assault on the city in 1400–01. Tamerlane turned his forces loose and permitted unprecedented plunder, murder and rape, citing the city's alleged persecution of the followers of 'Ali after the Battle of Kerbala seven centuries earlier as justification. An Italian visitor reached the city a few weeks later, and left an extraordinary account of the destruction, citing the Old Testament's Jeremiah: 'I will kindle a fire inside the walls of Damascus to devour the palaces of Ben-Hadad'. Tamerlane then deported the Syrian workmen and artists who had adorned the city's buildings and put them to work on the much grander (some would say more vulgar) buildings of the Mongol capital, Samarkand. It was another twenty years before new mosques or madrasas were built in Damascus.

One hopes contemporary Syria's reconstruction will be much more rapid. Only massive rebuilding will meet the basic needs of the millions who are now homeless. Outside assistance will be needed on a major scale. The country's archaeological and architectural heritage too will require a massive rescue effort. The international community will need to maintain measures already put into place, including through Interpol, for the interception of looted remains. It is unlikely that much of the material so far looted will find a market until fighting dies down.

There is one thing, though, the scholarly community outside Syria could consider in the interim. Much of our knowledge of Syria's past is still to be published. Many teams publish promptly or at least put out useful accounts of their seasons' outcomes on the Internet. Some, however, are obsessed by the need to keep information uncovered in digs away from the prying eyes of others. There is a risk that if digs are not resumed, all this raw material will be lost.

Moreover, the material in Syrian official collections is imperfectly recorded and rarely available to outsiders. Syria had an excessively rigid policy on the taking of photos in museums, rarely allowing informal recording of material for reference purposes, even without flash or tripod. If material has been looted from important collections, such informally gathered images could be invaluable either in tracing losses or tracking contraband material offered for sale abroad. While a central clearing house for such material is probably beyond any single institution's resources, all records easily scanned or digitised, including cataloguing data, should be put up on readily accessible websites by the various research institutions abroad that have operated in Syria. Not everything will be recovered in future years, but it is also important to know what has been lost amid Syria's vast treasure house, the world's greatest 'open museum'.

OLD DAMASCUS

Brigid Waddams

It feels very strange to be writing about a place that might not exist by the time you read this. So far the old city of Damascus has survived the Syrian conflict because the opposition fighters have not taken the battle into its streets and alleyways – but the moment they do, the regime will respond with bombs and shells, as they have done in Aleppo where tragically, so much of the old town has been destroyed.

Damascus still exists on a wing and a prayer. But in areas not far from the old city walls there is devastation: Jobar, for instance, where one of the oldest synagogues in the world was located, has been destroyed. The synagogue was famous for its beautiful old silver torah cases; it is said that Elijah is supposed to have anointed Elisha as his successor there. A strange story appeared in an Israeli paper last year claiming that before shells finally destroyed the synagogue, Israeli commandos had gone into Syria, grabbed these and other treasures and taken them back to Israel. I have no idea whether this story is true or not.

Damascus is a city that is doubly precious: it is the oldest continuously inhabited town in the world, which means that it is really a vast unexplored archaeological site. Every time they repair a drain or a pipe in Damascus they find a Roman arch, an amphitheatre, an ancient fountain. Last time I was there, not long before the uprising began, I was shown a house where the owners, revamping the place, had just discovered that their home was really a small Greek temple with pillars and an altar!

The other reason Damascus is unique is that it is the largest assembly of old private houses in the Arab world – a huge sample book, if you like, of early domestic architecture. Istanbul and Cairo may have more important monuments, but Damascus has the most authentic old city that exists anywhere with about 8,500 houses (half the number recorded in the

Ottoman yearbook of 1900) still standing, many with wonderfully decorated interiors.

I became involved with Damascus – obsessed would be a better word – when my diplomat husband was posted to Syria in the early 1990s as EU ambassador. In those days the old city was a blank to most middle-class Syrians: they never went into it and never thought about the place. They had abandoned their old houses there in the early decades of the twentieth century when motor cars came into common use and social habits changed and new generations wanted to set up home separately from their parents; when it became harder to find servants; when people discovered (probably influenced by their French occupiers) that they could live far more comfortably in a centrally-heated flat or house outside the old city walls. The empty palaces were taken over by squatters, refugees and the poor – divided up with breeze-block partitions between many families.

I used to go there sometimes to shop in the Spice Souk, but I lived in the suburb of Mezzeh, alongside other diplomats. And then came my own private Damascus conversion. I was taken by a friend from church, an eccentric old English lady called Fatie, known to everyone who spent time in Damascus (sadly, she died in February this year) to look at a house that she had heard was for sale.

I was quite unprepared for what we would find as we walked down a dark alley and then through a little door set into an enormous old wooden gate: suddenly we were in a fountain courtyard full of sunshine, with the most astonishing mirrored, marbled, gilded, painted rooms that I had ever seen. Until that moment I had absolutely no idea of the glories that lay hidden behind the blank walls of the old city that I had been walking by for the past year. But the house, Beit Mujallid it was called, was in terrible condition, paintings were peeling, walls were bulging, marble mosaic floors were falling apart, some ceilings had collapsed, roofs were leaking. I tried to persuade my husband to sell our home in England and take it on instead, and when that failed I wrote an article on the house (with the photographer Tim Beddow) for *The World of Interiors*. Nora Jumblatt, the wife of Druze leader Walid Jumblatt, who is herself a Damascene, saw the article, came from Lebanon to look at Beit Mujallid, and ended up buying it. She spent years, and a great deal of money, lovingly restoring the house with the help of conservators from the Louvre museum, but it has not been easy for her: when it was almost finished she was banned from Damascus for a couple of years because of remarks made by her husband about President Bashaar al-Assad. And now the Syrian regime has confiscated the house on the preposterous grounds that it should be turned into a cultural centre. There are dozens of other equally beautiful houses in Damascus crying out to be restored and turned into cultural centres.

It seemed to me when I first saw Beit Mujallid that Damascus was in the greatest danger it had ever faced, not from conquering armies or plague or pestilence but just from neglect. It would simply fall down because nobody cared. Though with hindsight, it was probably the neglect and poverty of the old city that saved it from being pulled down and redeveloped through the 1960 and 1970s. Tim Beddow and I decided to produce a book on the Old City to try and raise concern for its wonderful old houses. I bought a small tumble-down house behind the Great Mosque and restored it to encourage others to do the same. (Well, that was one of the reasons, but the real one was that I had fallen in love with Damascus and like anyone in love I wanted to be with my loved one, to belong, and not be just a daytime visitor.) The oddest thing about this is that I was only able to do it because, out of the blue, a relative I had never met died, and left me and my sister some money. My share was the exact amount I needed to buy a small and decrepit house.

They say that once you have lived in Damascus, Damascus lives in you, and I was certainly not the first foreign woman to fall in love with the place: Jane Digby, the scandalous British aristocrat who travelled to Syria in 1853, fell in love with an Arab Sheikh twenty years younger than herself, bought two houses in Damascus and never left. She is buried in the Protestant cemetery there. Her biographer Mary S. Lovell went to Damascus to research her, and found herself as much enchanted by the place as her subject. The archaeologist Freya Stark was equally bewitched: 'there is a magic, not to be understood in a day or even two', she declared, 'I am in love with the enchanted city'. But my favourite among the smitten ladies is Isobel Burton, the wife of Richard, the famous writer and explorer who was British Consul in Syria in 1869. When her husband was recalled, partly because his efforts to clean up money-lending rackets upset too many powerful factions in the city, Isobel wrote that the afternoon before she heard the news that they were obliged to leave, was her 'last happy day'. I remember feeling pretty much the same when our turn came to depart.

I identify with Isobel because she cared so much about the old city. She worried that newly-rich Yusuf Anbar was building his house in the wrong way. 'It is in more modern style', she wrote, 'and therefore less pleasing to me.' She was highly critical of the fact that he was buying up the old houses around his property and demolishing them to gain more space for his building. 'Unhappily he is also burning their carved wood and ancient ornaments in which he sees no grace and beauty, and laughs at me for my heartache.' Isobel far preferred Beit Lisbouna, a palace she contrasted with the Anbar house as being 'tasteful as well as old'. Lisbouna was still a beautiful house though in need of much repair when we were posted to Damascus 120 years later, and so was the vast Anbar palace, which now houses the administration of the old city. And that is one of the things I loved about Damascus, that it was constant, unchanging. As Ross Burns writes in his history of Damascus, 'traditional life continues in the old city with a matter-of-fact air that makes light of the centuries.'

Mark Twain put it more grandly: 'to Damascus years are only moments, decades are only flitting trifles of time. She measures time not by days, months and years but by the empires she has seen rise and prosper and crumble to ruin. She is a type of immortality. She saw Greece rise and flourish for two thousand years, and die. In her old age she saw Rome built, she saw it overshadow the world with its power; she saw it perish.... She has looked upon the dry bones of a thousand empires and will see the tombs of a thousand more before she dies.'

Let us pray and hope that Twain's words hold true and that this legendary and unique city comes out of the Syrian conflict unscathed.

VIRTUAL INTERACTIONS

Hania Mourtada

Before I started covering the war in Syria from a remote location, I was aware that reporters relied heavily on Skype and social media to cover the crisis. But only when I was in this position myself did I really come to understand how problematic Skype can be as a tool, how intimate relationships, through which a current of tension is always running, inevitably develop over time and infuse every interaction with a flood of emotions. In one Skype room, an intertwined virtual world of reporters, citizen-journalists, military council spokespeople, activists, smugglers, common criminals and fighters can be found.

When you're in a conflict zone, physically, you and the people on the ground are undergoing the same painful experience. If there's an airstrike, you experience it in real time. You don't watch the clip afterward, talk to a person who witnessed it, write something peppered with quotes gleaned from several Skype chat rooms, then close your laptop and move on with your day. There's no disconnect when you're in Syria. There are no two parallel realities loosely tied together by an internet connection. The best way to cover the conflict is to be there. Having said that, not everyone is brave enough to embrace the considerable risks, and as the conflict becomes more volatile, and al-Qaeda-affiliated groups gain ground, it has become increasingly more difficult to cross into Syria.

When you try to delve into people's daily realities over Skype, it engenders several problems. Reporting via Skype also means you are everywhere at once. You are keeping an eye on every Syrian province and every Syrian town. You are accessible to all citizen-journalists on your contact list and each one of your contacts, who is in a specific town, a tiny spot on the Syrian map, expects you to give them your undivided attention. And, more often than not, which story you decide to focus on on a given day is a question of timing and chance. If you're writing a news story, there is not enough space to cover everything that unravelled in Syria that day. Being in a position to pick one story over another, means you have all the power even though you're not even physically there. This can, at times, breed resentment from rebels and activists on the ground, who risk their lives to bring you the facts and the images without any guarantee that you will choose to tell their community's story.

At one point, a realisation struck me. The ongoing discourse that occurs in chat rooms between 'recognised' journalists who have a platform for their words and citizen-journalists who struggle to be heard is heightening the disempowerment felt by most Syrians. They tell us their stories and then it is up to us to discard them or give them a blurb in the next news story. It's tragic in every sense of the word.

The effect of this on Syrians became clear to me when I was made privy to a peculiar conversation between a brigade's spokesperson and a Syrian female journalist who works for a well-known news organisation. I was speaking to a young man based in Deir ez-Zor who is the official spokesman for the military council there. He witnesses battles, films them, reports on them and then delivers the neatly pre-packaged information to journalists working in Western news organisations (such as myself) sitting at the other end of a computer screen. Because I'm Syrian, he has always considered me his ally and, I believe, he is under the illusion that I'm a Sunni because he feels I'm on his 'side'. I am in fact a Shia Muslim, a minority sect deemed on the side of embattled president Bashaar al-Assad.

One day we were talking about Deir ez-Zor when suddenly he broke out of his serious persona and told me, 'so guess what, this Alawite Syrian girl who's a reporter for this news organisation is telling me her two cousins are trapped in the military base my brigade is about to attack'. He's the spokesman of an anti-regime brigade fighting to topple Bashaar al-Assad. She's an Alawite Syrian journalist who talks to him on a regular basis to get the details she needs to write her stories. On that day, she found out that the military base this young man's brigade was besieging was the same one where her cousins, who serve in the army, had been deployed. Suddenly the situation shifted for both actors. It was no longer the citizen-journalist/fighter pleading with the big shot reporter to make his voice heard. This time, she was hysterically begging him to convince his brigade to spare her young cousins' lives. What was most unsettling about the experience for me was that he seemed to thoroughly enjoy this sudden turn of events where, for once, he felt he had the upper hand. He was so euphoric he felt the need for someone to bear witness to this sudden and cruel reversal of fates. He copy pasted their entire personal chat for me to read.

As I read the long thread, I realised that in a peculiar convergence of two parallel worlds, I was plunged deep into the intertwined personal lives of two people I had never met. Those two individuals had forged a solid friendship and she was trying to tell his story to the world. But in Syria, on the ground, the brigade he represents in the media was about to kill her Alawite cousins. There was a definite power shift. As a mere spokesman he probably had no say in what would happen to her young cousins who were forced to serve in the army but he acted as if he did. He asked her abrupt questions like 'do they have blood on their hands?' She swore one of them was mentally challenged and had been forcibly conscripted and that neither one of them ever wanted to be in the army. He sneered and mocked her and made light of the tragic situation. Because in that moment, he was her only source of knowledge about what might happen to her cousins, he let his resentment come to the surface. The girl, who was otherwise on very good terms with him, was shocked that he expressed no sympathy whatsoever. Being privy to their private conversation, which I knew I wasn't supposed to read, was a very unsettling experience for me as a Syrian. Interactions on Skype are simultaneously divorced from reality and yet very much rooted in something real.

It is easy to feel disheartened at what has befallen my country. Sanitised virtual spaces, which allow us to delve deep into all the layers of the conflict, and the simplistic overarching narrative we reluctantly construct once we fail to cement all the layers, leave me feeling like I have failed my countrymen and women. Much of the crisis remains enigmatic but, for me, there will always be a palpable beauty in the juxtaposition of the fragmented conversations that have come to characterise the upheaval. It is an invigorated political culture characterised by truth-telling, however fragmented it may be. We Syrians all fear a legacy of bitterness that will keep reproducing itself indefinitely, a scenario akin to Lebanon's travails.

The technology at our disposal allows us Syrians to reach out to each other beyond the cloistered communities we have sought refuge in. This sometimes answers the question 'what could it look like when all of this is over?'

The young man's responses betrayed a fickle and transient manifestation of empathy. In moments of weakness, he seemed to cave in and comfort his friend. Yet his tone hardened because he was intent on victimising those he had come to think of as victimisers. In that moment, clarity was supplanted by 'I am a righteous Sunni whose rights have been trampled on by the likes of her, the alien Alawites we can't coexist with anymore'. Still, I could look beyond his callousness and feel a stirring in his conscience. Sustained enmity toward a group perceived as the cause of all ills can be draining to uphold, and I can sometimes see this fatigue settling in among fighters. Journalists covering the conflict should not forget that the reality outside their door has been momentarily suspended while on the other end, it continues to rage in the background. What transpires in closed private chat rooms can have direct bearings on the ground and vice versa.

Syrians left to their miserable fate have come to feel that they are the last to be involved when the destiny of their country is being debated. As the initial euphoria of breaking free dissipates, fatigue has weakened their resolve. The frontline shifts again and again but nothing else seems to change. Within the confines of these Skype rooms and social media accounts, they sense that they have at least a measure of control over the grotesque images that are circulating at their expense.

With the beginning of the uprising, we saw a visible return to artistic content that is much more transgressive and political. The monopoly over artistic creation shifted from the established dissident man of letters, whose voice remained rather absent in the context of the popular revolt, to the average Syrian who has no artistic credentials to speak of but is in possession of a laptop.

There was an extraordinary, almost instant move to reclaim the field of dissident cultural production initiated by civil activists and anonymous artists. The uprising has revolutionised the cultural and artistic field of political truth-telling even as it drove it underground. One of the most notable transformations is a nascent type of prison narrative which stands apart, in content and form, from the conventional prison narratives written by Syrian authors in the past two decades. The new prison narratives seek to demystify the experience of imprisonment and torture in attempts to portray the power of the regime as surmountable. Describing what prison is like is now a prescriptive act rather than a descriptive venture. The usual sense of resignation and passive resistance in older prison narratives is supplanted by a defiant invigorated spirit and a 'triumph against all odds' rhetoric. Humour is evident in all accounts. The grim, metaphorical truth-telling of the 1980s and 1990s is gradually replaced by a more optimistic forward-looking language. It may be that this altered ethos, which no longer just seeks to expose and resist power but also to overcome it, is another starting point from which to examine the new political spirit, however fragmented, of the Syrian uprising.

ISBN: 9781849044004
£20.00 / Hardback / 240pp

AMONG THE RUINS

SYRIA PAST AND PRESENT

CHRISTIAN C. SAHNER

As a civil war shatters a country and consumes its people, historian Christian Sahner offers a poignant account of Syria, where the past profoundly shapes its dreadful present.

Among the Ruins blends history, memoir and reportage, drawing on the author's extensive knowledge of Syria in ancient, medieval, and modern times, as well as his experiences living in the Levant on the eve of the war and in the midst of the 'Arab Spring'. These plotlines converge in a rich narrative of a country in constant flux — a place renewed by the very shifts that, in the near term, are proving so destructive.

Sahner focuses on five themes of interest to anyone intrigued and dismayed by Syria's fragmentation since 2011: the role of Christianity in society; the arrival of Islam; the rise of sectarianism and competing minorities; the emergence of the Ba'ath Party; and the current pitiless civil war.

Among the Ruins is a brisk and illuminating read, an accessible introduction to a country with an enormously rich past and a tragic present. For anyone seeking to understand Syria, this book should be their starting point.

'*Among the Ruins* is a uniquely vivid evocation of the past of Syria and a prescient record of its present state. Deeply humane and drawing on subjects from all walks of life, Sahner has a gift for presenting them against a past that is as varied and as ancient as the country itself. We are brought to the edge of the precipice over which, alas, a magnificently diverse society appears to have stumbled. We will be both better informed and wiser for reading it.' — Peter Brown, Rollins Professor Emeritus of History at Princeton University

WWW.HURSTPUBLISHERS.COM/BOOK/AMONG-THE-RUINS

41 GREAT RUSSELL ST, LONDON WC1B 3PL
WWW.HURSTPUBLISHERS.COM
WWW.FBOOK.COM/HURSTPUBLISHERS
020 7255 2201

VOLUNTEERS AND TERRORISTS

Boyd Tonkin

Whenever the BBC needs a familiar standby to fill a gap in its early-evening schedules, it turns to 'Dad's Army'. As a result, David Croft and Jimmy Perry's much-loved Second World War sitcom has over the decades tickled audiences a lot younger than those who saw the nine series on their first outings between 1968 and 1977. The Home Guard volunteers of Walmington-on-Sea have become bona fide national treasures, with the show's quirky comedy of character immeasurably deepened by our knowledge that – for a time – the real-life equivalents of these bumbling oldies did indeed stand in the front line of defence against genocidal fascism.

The Home Guard or Local Defence Volunteers, given official status by an Order in Council on 17 May 1940 and stood down on 31 December 1945, had a remarkable birth. As fears of a German invasion grew in 1940, the force's architect had to fight his own campaign against the scorn and suspicion of military top brass and cautious politicians alike. But his idea for decentralised self-defence militias caught on fast. By July 1940, it had attracted 1.5 million volunteers across the country. Not only did the Home Guard stiffen morale at a time when Britain had no European allies against Hitler; its members took an active part in conflict by manning anti-aircraft batteries and downing many Luftwaffe planes.

Tom Wintringham, the visionary strategist who had agitated for a Home Guard since 1938, outraged the Colonel Blimps with his polemic 'How to Reform the Army'. He kick-started support for 'people's militias' when he opened a Home Guard training school in guerrilla warfare at Osterley. The authorities tried (and failed) to shut down this nest of 'Marxist hooligans', but its principles had already taken root. Always the maverick, Wintringham never secured a regular army commission. In 1942, he founded the left-of-Labour Common Wealth party. But what would have happened to the oddball soldier who inspired home-front warriors today? He could have been subject to a sentence of imprisonment for life.

Then a member of the Communist Party, Wintringham had commanded the British Battalion of the International Brigades at the Battle of Jarama in February 1937. At 'Suicide Hill', through an extraordinary combination of pluck and luck, the British volunteers played a bloodily decisive role in the early stages of the Spanish Civil War. They were instrumental in holding back Franco's rebel forces in their advance on Madrid and so helped safeguard the capital for the legal Republican government. Although Madrid would ultimately fall in 1939, Jarama arguably counts as the most significant battlefield rebuff for international fascism until the Battle of El Alamein in November 1942. But the human cost to the exposed British contingent proved enormous. In *Unlikely Warriors*, his definitive recent account of British and Irish fighters in the Spanish Civil War, Richard Baxell calculates that 'Of the 630 men who had gone into action on 12 February, only 80 were left unscathed when the battle ended three days later'.

Heroes? Not, since 2006, according to British law. Some 2,300 British volunteers fought against Franco in Spain; more than 500 were killed. Although history tends to remember the writers and intellectuals – George Orwell and John Cornford, Ralph Fox and Laurie Lee – most were working-class trade unionists in their late twenties, with almost 200 Welsh miners among them. Memorials up and down the land now hail their sacrifice for freedom. In 1996, the government of Spain put a seal on their contribution by proposing an offer of citizenship to every surviving soldier of the International Brigades.

A decade after that, and just before the grant of citizenship to all veterans entered Spanish law, Tony Blair's third administration passed the Terrorism Act 2006. Section Five, as currently interpreted by the Crown Prosecution Service, makes it an offence to take part in military action abroad with a 'political, ideological, religious or racial motive'. The legislation appears to forbid all training or action in a foreign combat – not merely to overthrow a tyranny, but also to sustain a democracy at risk. If so, its provisions would have criminalised every Briton who fought in Spain. It would have turned Lord Byron, whose commitment to Greek independence led him to arm and lead a raggle-taggle regiment prior to his death at Missolonghi in 1824, into an outlaw. As for the 6,500 veterans of Wellington's armies who went off after Waterloo to fight against Spanish colonial rule in the battles that led to the independence of Colombia, Venezuela and Ecuador, and whom Simon Bolivar the Liberator called 'salvadores di mi patria', how could the courts and prisons have processed such a lawless throng?

In January 2014, sixteen Britons were arrested after returning from Syria. Although the 2006 legislation galloped through parliament in the wake of the 7/7 bombings in London, it now targets UK citizens deemed to have fought with the myriad of Syrian rebel groups. Estimates of the number of British fighters vary wildly but a figure of around 400 has gained currency. At least eight have died. The fear of radicalisation, with any link to al-Qaeda-allied units treated as a communicable virus, has propelled the hard legal line.

Sue Hemming, head of counter-terrorism at the Crown Prosecution Service, has made it perfectly clear that the pursuit of British volunteers in Syria does not count as the unintended consequence of a statute meant to address other evils. 'Potentially it's an offence to go out and get involved in a conflict, however loathsome you think the people on the other side are,' she affirms (*Evening Standard*, 3 February 2014). 'Our government chooses to have legislation which prevents people from joining in whichever conflicts they have views about. We will apply the law robustly.'

Of course, howling ironies surrounds this legislation. Now it pursues people who unofficially assist an objective – the military impairment of the Assad regime – that the UK government sought until its parliamentary defeat in August 2013. On 6 February, in the best-known case so far of British volunteer involvement, Waheed Majeed from Martyrs Avenue in Crawley, West Sussex, drove an explosive-packed truck at the gates of Aleppo jail to become the first suicide attacker from this country to die in Syria. His brother Hafeez claimed that 'My brother was not a terrorist. My brother was a hero'. If he had been a British soldier and assailed an Assad torture-factory- a far-from-impossible notion last summer – 'he would have been awarded the posthumous Victoria Cross'.

We need not whitewash the motives and methods of the al-Nusra front, the Islamic State of Iraq and al-Sham, or other jihadi groupings which may seek to recruit UK travellers to Syria. No doubt their commanders and ideologists would love to re-export the idea of sacred violence as far as possible via a 'blowback' effect. Yet UK policy-makers, police and security agencies have chosen to view Syria exclusively through the lens of 'radicalisation', and the medical analogy of contamination and contagion that comes with it. That may blur their view of the emotions and experiences of young men whose future paths worry the authorities so much.

Here the Spanish Civil War precedent may prove far from trivial. The International Brigaders espoused noble ideals. Yet, as participants such as Orwell and Arthur Koestler quickly made plain, they did not serve a uniformly noble hierarchy. The Brigades' ever-closer integration into the Comintern and Soviet foreign-policy aims compromised its democratic credentials. Some dissidents – Orwell among them – distrusted the incorporation of the Brigades into a sort of Stalinist International. Homage to Catalonia records his disillusioned anger with the takeover of the conduct of the war by cynical proxies of Moscow. Orwell had chosen to fight with POUM, the autonomous revolutionary militia treated as an unruly Trotskyist splinter by the Brigades' leadership.

'Objectively', to use that favourite bargaining-chip of 1930s political argument, British and other volunteers may have helped the broader interests of a far-from benign Soviet policy. Subjectively, save for an atypical handful of true ideologues, they generally took up arms for liberty and in solidarity with a threatened people. Any neutral observer might imagine that their trajectory – fully documented in memoirs, interviews, films and histories – should have guided official reactions when young British men again began to journey overseas to help, and perhaps to fight. For in Syria, just as in Spain, the border between humanitarian assistance and military combat has turned out to be distinctly porous.

The Spanish parallel proves instructive on another level too. The Brigaders hardly came back to a heroes' welcome. Wintringham's frustration, as the Colonel Blimps kept him out of the army in spite of his proven gifts of leadership, was commonplace for returned volunteers. Secret documents show that, before and after the outbreak of war in September 1939, recruiters were told to treat service in Spain as a marker of potential disloyalty. Richard Baxell quotes one veteran, John Peet, who learned that 'all applications for commissions in the armed forces are being screened by the Special Branch at Scotland Yard to keep out anybody who has actually been through a modern war' – i.e., the International Brigaders.

In 1939, the Communist connection alarmed the authorities as much as an al-Qaeda link these days. Although a couple of veterans did try to spy for the Soviet Union, these fears were mostly misplaced. Exposure to the Comintern power-grab in Republican Spain, followed by fury at the Nazi-Soviet Pact of 1938, had loosened the ties of many fighters to the party. Experience had turned them against their would-be foreign controllers. Might such a chain of events unwind in Syria?

Given Britain's plight in 1940, the blanket ban on Spanish veterans could not last. Some won commissions and many more soon served in the ranks. Bill Alexander, the final commander of the British Battalion and a Communist who stuck with the party, did his officer training at Sandhurst in 1942. He passed out first in his year before becoming a tank captain in North Africa, Italy and Germany. However, routine suspicion and sometimes discrimination persisted. When he learned about battle-hardened ex-comrades from Spain wasted on backroom tasks despite their front-line expertise, Tom Wintringham wrote scathingly that 'I sometimes wonder if the powers that run this country are determined to lose this war in their own way and without interference'.

Young people volunteer for foreign combat from a variety of reasons. Heartfelt belief in the justice of their cause fires many, as does solidarity with those of a similar background or outlook. For others, a simple itch for adventure or boredom with their life at home will supply the necessary push. From Wellington's grizzled veterans in the Andes through to the last-ditch defenders at Jarama, British history gives us ample opportunities to understand the urge to go abroad to fight.

Today's security-led prism, and the automatic penalties it envisages for any returnee, appears blind to all nuance and thus – objectively – both unwise and unjust. According to one report, a British volunteer with ISIS – one of the most extreme of the units – tweeted a poster that read 'Keep Calm, Support ISIS': a spoof of the already much-parodied Second World War campaign to beef up domestic morale. What are the chances that the kid who wrote that poster had watched Dad's Army? Pretty high, I would imagine. If so, he will be many things apart from a bloodthirsty future avenger dedicated to importing Syrian-style mayhem into British streets.

Neither is the long-term significance of such an overseas commitment apparent at the time. In late October 1938, on the eve of their dissolution, the surviving International Brigades marched through Barcelona. In a resonant address, the Communist deputy and orator Dolores Ibarruri – La Pasionaria – paid tribute to 'the courage, the sacrifice, the daring, the discipline of the men of the International Brigades'. 'You can go proudly,' she told them. 'You are history. You are legend. You are the heroic example of democracy's solidarity and universality'. Later writers often quote that speech as if La Pasionaria were voicing routine pieties. At that moment, though, much of Europe would have flatly contradicted her. As she asked women to tell their children about the heroism of the Brigades in an era 'when the rancours have died out and pride in a free country is felt equally by all Spaniards', her gamble on the future must have sounded fanciful. Yet, after a long night, that day did break. Only in 2007, sixty-nine years later, did the law on citizenship for foreign veterans pass.

One can't expect police officers and security operatives to gaze too far into futurity. Politicians might wish to take a slightly longer view. Instead, every volunteer in Syria now knows that they will return with an invisible brand marked 'potential murderer' stamped on them by the agencies of surveillance. In a BBC radio analysis last autumn, one British fighter known as 'Abu Muhadjar' thought it a 'slightly surreal' notion to 'go back to UK and start a jihad there'. For him at least, 'As to the global jihad, I couldn't tell you if I'm going to be alive tomorrow let alone future plans.'

Just because you hear someone rashly cry 'wolf' does not mean that wolves don't exist. Jihadi recruiters have no doubt got to work in Syria on some impressionable outsiders. In that case, surely the dogmatic assumption of malice implicit in Sue Hemming's warning would only strengthen their hand. If the threat of UK criminal sanctions blocks off your route to swift re-integration, then why not rise to the extremists' bait? What have you got to lose if your country's laws reward your commitment – however confused – with the label of terrorism?

Not many saints went from Britain to the Spanish Civil War – but not many thugs either. For many recruits in both Spain and Syria, idealism, escapism and sheer youthful bravado will have been pretty evenly mixed.

After such an episode, you would expect young men to develop in many different ways.

The Spanish volunteers certainly did. One veteran of the International Brigades became a champion of neo-liberal economics and an ideological mentor to Margaret Thatcher: Sir Alfred Sherman. Another would become Britain's most prominent, moderate and mainstream, trade-union chief: Jack Jones. A third would quit all political activism to flourish as a fruitily eccentric character actor: James Robertson Justice. It is hard to imagine a better way to kill off such variously productive careers than by tainting every young adventurer, whatever their motives, with a lifelong criminal stigma.

'The mountains look on Marathon,' rhymed Lord Byron before he took up arms in a foreign conflict, 'And Marathon looks on the sea;/ And musing there an hour alone,/ I dream'd that Greece might still be free;/ For standing on the Persians' grave,/ I could not deem myself a slave.' Not a slave, My Lord – but, under Section Five, most probably a terrorist.

ISBN: 9781849043014
£16.99 / Paperback / 288pp

Medina in Birmingham, Najaf in Brent

Inside British Islam

INNES BOWEN

Muslim intellectuals may try to define something called British Islam, but the truth is that as the Muslim community of Britain has grown in size and religiosity, so too has the opportunity to found and run mosques which divide along ethnic and sectarian lines.

Just as most churches in Britain are affiliated to one of the main Christian denominations, the vast majority of Britain's 1600 mosques are linked to wider sectarian networks: the Deobandi and Tablighi Jamaat movements with their origins in colonial India; the Salafi groups inspired by an austere form of Islam widely practiced in Saudi Arabia; the Islamist movements with links to religious political parties in the Middle East and South Asia; the Sufi movements that tend to emphasise spirituality rather than religious and political militancy; and the diverse Shi'ite sects which range from the orthodox disciples of Grand Ayatollah Sistani in Iraq to the Ismaili followers of the pragmatic and modernising Aga Khan. These affiliations are usually not apparent to outsiders, but inside Britain's Muslim communities sectarian divides are often fiercely guarded by religious leaders.

This book, of which no equivalent volume yet exists, is a definitive guide to the ideological differences, organisational structures and international links of the main Islamic groups active in Britain today.

'After a decade of fear-mongering, when Islam was portrayed as a unitary threat to the West, here comes a book that cuts through the hysteria. In this short and very readable volume, Bowen shows the complexity and nuances of Islam in Britain. This is a must-read for all people who want to understand the changing nature of Britain and its Muslim communities.' — Marc Sageman, author of *Leaderless Jihad: Terror Networks in the Twenty-First Century*

WWW.HURSTPUBLISHERS.COM/BOOK/MEDINA-IN-BIRMINGHAM-NAJAF-IN-BRENT

41 GREAT RUSSELL ST, LONDON WC1B 3PL
WWW.HURSTPUBLISHERS.COM
WWW.FBOOK.COM/HURSTPUBLISHERS
020 7255 2201

ARTS AND LETTERS

SYRIA'S TROJAN WOMEN

Itab Azzam

It is October 2013. I am in the back of a Jordanian taxi, national radio pumping out all our adoration of the Hashemite dynasty, searching for the tower blocks and alleyways where the Syrian refugees live. I am going to convince them to be part of a theatre workshop. I know it's not going to be an easy job.

No one acts in Syria. Certainly no one outside a jealously guarded inner circle of the equally exclusive secular elite, and I wasn't going to find many of them living six or seven to a room in Amman. Most of the families who fled the war and are now surviving as refugees in Jordan are members of Syria's deprived and voiceless majority. I also knew that in the towns and villages they called home, a woman doesn't expose a hair on her head outside the house, let alone bare their souls on stage to a bunch of foreigners.

Two months earlier a mutual friend had put me in touch with Charlotte Eagar. We met in leafy Kensington, London, amidst the spoils of her garlanded career as a foreign correspondent at the *Sunday Times* and *The Observer*. She'd given all this up to join her husband and partner, Willy Stirling, in a project to reinvent themselves as film producers. Their plan was to follow up the success of their first film, *Scooterman*, with a re-imagination on stage and screen of their great passion, the tragedy of Euripides, through the eyes of the women of Syria.

Back in the 1990s Charlotte was dodging bullets in Bosnia when she heard a BBC radio production of the *Trojan Women*, a play Euripides had written in 415 BC, the year after his fellow Athenians had laid waste the Aegean island of Melos, murdered every male inhabitant and taken the women and children prisoner to serve them as slaves. As a distant mirror to the horror of his own times, Euripides held up the suffering of the mythical women of Troy. Some 2,400 years later in 1992, Charlotte had seen in that same mirror a reflection of scenes she had witnessed in the Balkan wars. And now the same thing was happening where I come from, Syria.

Nine weeks later we were out there trying to make it happen. My co-producer Hal and I had only to find a theatre, a rehearsal venue, a director, an acting trainer, a writer, and at least thirty scared and vulnerable women prepared to trust us to transform them over six weeks into the queens and princesses of ancient Troy.

Oxfam provided us with a list of women, selected according to some mysterious, possibly entirely absent, logic, who they thought might be interested in the project. I called some of the Syrian activists working in Jordan and Hal and I decided to camp out outside the UNHCR registration centre, as it was a good place to meet many Syrians queuing to be registered.

The first family we met were living in Sahab, an unsafe area on the outskirts of Amman. The family described it as a 'drug land'. Maysoon had fled from the suburbs of Damascus with her two sisters and their families after her husband, a former officer in the Syrian army, defected and joined the Free Syrian Army.

Despite what they'd been through, they were all jokes and open minds. When pushed, though, Maysoon admitted their lives were painfully empty. She had lost her job and her home and she had been forced to marry her daughter off to a man twice her age. They had no money. She was feeling numb and completely broken. But she loved the idea of the play. She told me she could see it would give her an opportunity to speak her mind and engage her soul. Maysoon and her sisters never missed a day in the workshop and threw themselves wholeheartedly into every minute.

We spent two weeks forcing down litres of sugary tea and coffee, trying to bring around woman after woman to the project, and of course their husbands. This resistance was always inevitable. Arabs everywhere might lap up the soaps and costume dramas churned out by the Damascus studios, but away from the red carpets of the capital, in Syria's rickety suburbs and villages, it is a different prospect for a woman to put herself in the spotlight. There are dangerous implications of mingling with strange men and, worse still, exposing yourself to crowds of them in public. How, also, was a wife and mother going to keep putting food on the table and clean clothes on their children's backs, hard enough under the circumstances, with this added distraction?

The women themselves were obviously enticed. They liked that someone, a great playwright even, thought women's suffering worth writing about, and to be asked by these exotic newcomers to add their own voices. And that couldn't help but turn their heads just a little. But still a lot of women found it hard to believe that acting in a play was likely to change anything in their lives; and as time went on even I began to lose faith that it would.

I left Syria in 2011. I had been back once or twice, and I'd seen the situation around my family deteriorate. But we, thank God, have been spared the worst of it. In Jordan, in just a few days, I visited scores of families devastated in some of the worst ways imaginable. I sat for hours with families no different to mine, but in these families there were gaps where brothers, fathers, mothers, children once sat. And those who had made it to these sad lodgings were only telling me part of what the bereavements, the destitution, and the rapes had done to them. As each day passed, the more our noble goals seemed to fade into insignificance. What was I doing there trying to convince people to be in a play when all they needed was a blanket? Emptily, I tried to explain the psychological value of participating in such a project, but the truth is their focus was on how to survive till tomorrow.

According to the UNHCR, Jordan had received some 600,000 Syrian refugees by March 2014. In Amman, tens of thousands Syrian families are living in tiny flats with tin roofs: no heating in winter, no light, no nothing. Most of them do illegal work and live in endless fear of deportation back to Syria, with only the brutality of a merciless regime to meet them.

We were offering six weeks in a room doing vocal exercises and reading an ancient Greek play.

Still, after seeing over seventy women I managed somehow to convince twenty-five to come to the rehearsals. I said to them, 'just come on the first day and see whether you like it or not'. The clincher for most of them was the safe neutral venue – a community centre – that we found for rehearsals and the nursery for their children; it would have been impossible without it. In the first few days we had children running around while their mothers compared notes on how they'd fled Syria.

Everyone's darling was Sham, three-months old and good as gold, the
company mascot, who somehow slept through the sack of Troy and the
rampages of the Greek army day after day. Where I come from, we believe
in past lives, and I have no doubt she'd been in the theatre before. Her
mother wanted so desperately to be part of the play she would be breast-
feeding her in the break or between rehearsals.

We started with exercises. The women loved it. 'What could be better
than free exercise?' they winked. Nanda Mohammed, the acting trainer,
went through her repertoire of rehearsal games, the first any of them had
played since childhood. Playground rivalry instantly set in jokes and banter.
They had a go at designing their own costumes alongside Bissan Al Charif,
the set designer. Of course most of them came up with perfect eighteenth
century Disney princess dresses. It was not an easy thing to let them down
on that one.

We were all taken aback by the passions we had unleashed. There was hardly a late arrival, let alone a no-show. They loved it so much that they refused to miss rehearsals, even on days when a biblical snowstorm put Amman on hold. For them it was more than a play, it was a lifetime achievement. They wanted to do it well.

And at the end, of course, lay the terrifying and exhilarating thought of the performance.

They wanted, with a passion that stunned even me, to send a message, to tell their own stories in their own voice. And they felt appreciated. They felt important. For the first time in their lives they were being asked to do something intellectually challenging. They were given the freedom to say whatever they wanted, and they found that their opinions mattered.

The workshop helped them organise their thoughts. Helped them feel energised and alive again. 'I have something to wake up for in the morning', Raneem told me.

In the last week of the workshop, Nadine came up to me with teary eyes and said 'This is the best thing that happened to me in my entire life'. I asked her why. 'Because I feel human again'. And they weren't the only ones affected. No one walked away from those six weeks unchanged. Working with those women gave me a different perspective on my own country; it also changed my perspective on the war itself.

For the first eighteen years of my life I grew up in a village near Sweida, a predominantly Druze province in the south of Syria. My parents weren't rich, but they were liberal and secular. Opportunities to mingle freely with the women from the conservative villages near ours were few and far between. I went to study English in Damascus and it was there that, after graduation, I took my first steps in a media career. In the years that followed, I spent most of my time with liberals and wannabe bohemians like me. I look back fondly on those dreamy idealistic years, but with hindsight I see the price we paid was an ever-widening gap between our lives and horizons and those of ordinary Syrians.

In pre-revolutionary Syria a clear separation of class existed between the sophisticated educated elite and the rest. The cultural scene in Damascus and Aleppo, the two largest cities in Syria, was exclusive and detached. Time and time again, I came across attitudes that viewed the ordinary Syrian as a threat, an embarrassing non-initiate in the international art world whose acceptance the elite craved. I remember being haughtily denied funding to take a massively popular electro-folk band from Dara'a on a tour of Europe, but pointed in the direction of the national philharmonic. And the vaults of the National Film Organisation heaved with thoughtful films lauded on the festival circuit, which were never allowed to see the interior of a Syrian cinema.

All of this, of course, was part of an attitude and a strategy enacted with ruthless efficiency by the regime against its people. Who could wish the overthrow of these socially liberal and outward-looking people by uneducated, socially conservative peasants? Never mind that it was precisely those liberal people who kept the rest uneducated and impoverished. The average Syrian sensibly kept himself to himself. It's ironic that it took the horrific trauma of civil war to bring these distinctions to the fore.

Over six weeks of intensive training and activities, rare and beautiful cross-cultural friendships began to blossom between the theatre professionals and the ordinary women, who now had a shared goal as well as a shared exile. I enjoyed being transformed by them and watching them transform every day. Without a doubt the experience has enriched my life. Fatima, Maysoon, Nadine and the others gave the lie to every stereotype I have ever heard about conservative women. They were eager to learn, enthusiastic, and they broke barriers. They were strong, they were eloquent.

'In Syria we were looked down upon as hijabi women. Have you ever seen a hijabi presenter on TV or a hijabi actress? Never!' More than anything, Nadine told me, she was grateful that we gave hijabi women an opportunity to act.

I still sometimes find it hard to justify spending thousands of pounds on a theatre project while some Syrians are being starved to death. But projects like these bring genuine psychological help to a large group of people in a short and effective way, which in turn, we can only hope, will have a long-lasting effect on their and their families' well-being. Everything in a Syrian family revolves around the mother, and we want psychologically healthy, ambitious, fulfilled women to pass the benefits onto their children and therefore to society at large.

For me, the most important achievement is that we managed to bring theatre to a class of people that have never seen, never even read a play, let alone acted in one, a tiny rectification of a tiny fault representative of so many that was not theirs but the fault of Syrian society and the Syrian regime.

Finally, the women's ability to be at peace with each other despite deep differences in political opinion gave me new hope for Syria – not the Syria we live with today, torn this way and that between fighters arriving every day from Iran, Lebanon, London and Baghdad. We've lived with our own leaders and outsiders reminding us of our divisions, but it only takes a few weeks rehearsing a play to remember what makes us all human.

THE CHILDREN OF ATMEH CAMP

Tom Hill

Atmeh Camp, Idlib, Syria (Syrian-Turkish border), March 2013—'Where are you from?' Yaser of the Maram Foundation asks one of the dozens of children peering shyly at the gathering of teachers and aid workers come to formally 'inaugurate' *Madrasat al-Awda*: the 'School of Return': an affair of four small tents.

The little girl's name is Hania. She is no more than four years old and, like so many of over 10,000 children in Atmeh camp, is barefoot in the quagmire of mud. There are new arrivals every day, some days thousands at once from the latest village to suffer aerial bombing or shelling. When I visit, Hania is barely older than a conflict that just turned two years old. She will never remember anything before it began. Putting on a big smile, she, like so many of the other children, answers the question by reflexively pointing across the mud towards her tent. 'No—not where are you from in the camp!' Yaser responds, pained, not scolding: 'Where are you from in Syria?'

Like many in the camp, Hania is from Kafr Zeita, in the Hama countryside. Look it up on YouTube and the first result reads: 'Massacre in Hama—Kafr Zeita—Civilians Burned Alive.' The footage dates from June 2012, shortly after Hania and the other children and their families in this corner of the camp landed here, on the rolling slopes of an olive grove on the Syrian-Turkish border, without shelter, water or electricity, no school or health care, and no possibility of entering Turkey: the Turkish government has, for now, stopped letting these and some 100,000 other Internally Displaced Persons (IDPs) cross the border to become refugees. For sixty-five years Palestinian children in their own refugee camps have been taught to think and say they are not from the camp where they and their parents have spent their whole lives, but from the village they have never seen. It is far too soon to fear the same fate for Hania, but the echoes are foreboding.

Why did they come to Atmeh? In part, because it is likely one of the only relatively safe places in Syria, over the hills from the bombing of the regime's MiG fighter planes. The camp is just a few hundred metres across from the Turkish border, too close to be an inviting target for fear of diplomatic complications. But the hills can only muffle the near-constant shelling beyond them. Some days one hears it even from Reyhanlı, just across the border in Turkey. The road to Reyhanlı is staffed by a single Turkish soldier, but the refugee camps in Turkey, inadequate but featuring 'the highest standard of material aid we have ever seen in such a crisis' according to an EU official, might as well be a thousand miles away.

At least Hania hasn't lost the power of speech. Zeina is a year or two older—but she doesn't talk, much less smile, as she orbits the camp, grim-faced. Like most of the children here, she is 'working': trying perfunctorily to sell three packets of crisps from a cardboard box, uninterested in them herself, instead chewing on the plastic that barely holds her box together. Others, slightly older, sell local Alhamra cigarettes. To most questions, Zeina shakes her head and clucks 'no' like the adult she already is, from the height of her five years. During our week's visit she almost smiled once, but was prevented by her foreboding frowning. This wasn't directed, needless to say, at the foreigner pestering her (How could one buy her crisps at the 'school' without being surrounded by dozens more offering the same?) —but at two miniscule newborn puppies chewing a piece of something between them. Zeina has an older brother who drags her away by the collar from what's not for her—for example, the distribution of a few donated notebooks and pencils to the students of the school, that consists, for now, of the four small tents—and no furniture. She's from the 75 per cent of the camp's children who have only a makeshift school to go to.

When I visit, it is barely six months since Atmeh's Olive Tree camp was 'founded'. Yakzan Shishakly, a visiting Syrian-American with an air-conditioning company in Houston and no experience of humanitarian management, came across the first displaced families in this olive grove, and dropped his life to care for them. For now it has the distinction of being the biggest camp inside Syria. Yet it still suffers from several factors such as chronic overcrowding: one sample canvas tarpaulin tent housed eighteen members of one family. The camp is full of mud and disease, which will only get worse when the summer arrives, for lack of vaccines. Already, Shishakly says, 'we're really afraid of the summer'; of 'really long days', and 'we fear cholera'.

Girls in a classroom in the Return School, Atmeh Camp, Syria

Shishakly and his team have more pressing concerns than anyone can handle. Today, it is the functioning of the camp's new kitchen and the arrival of a desperately-needed new generator, paid for by a donation from the Gulf – tent fires have claimed several lives here. Tomorrow, a new 'women's tent' with a space for *tatriz* (embroidery) will be set up. As Shishakly walks through the camp, he is constantly approached for more tents but has to say no over and again.

Setting up something like a school has been uniquely urgent. The camp is its children, by far the most vulnerable victims of the conflict. Everywhere one turns they are carrying water, standing in line for the camp's only collective restroom, selling cigarettes, or just running around the tents. In that sense Atmeh is reminiscent of camps in Gaza—but it's even more crowded.

Only the Syrian government can authorise the full and unimpeded access of Damascus-based UN agencies to the millions of internally displaced persons (IDPs) in Syria, whether they are in camps like Atmeh or outside them—and of course it doesn't. Without this, an abstract 'return' is the best, if not the only, thing that those in Atmeh feel they can hope for. Here, the 'school' is, without furniture, materials or enough staff, largely devoted to singing revolutionary songs. This is an activity that costs nothing apart from the teachers' time, and lasts beyond the few hours a day in which the school functions. Long after sunset, one can hear the songs emerging from tents in every corner of the camp.

Lining up to collect the family's lentil soup ration from the camp kitchen, Atmeh

Already, the question of the camp's permanence looms large. It is dubbed 'one of the grimmest refugee camps in the world' or 'an abomination of a camp' in mainstream media reports. More than a camp, it is now a small city. It cannot compare in size to Za'atari, the city-camp in Jordan housing some 124,000 refugees who, crucially, have access to international aid, however inadequate. But even trying to count Atmeh camp's residents, never mind to provide adequately for them, is an impossible task: they were 5,000 in September, 8–12,000 two months ago. According to the Maram Foundation, they are now at least 18,000: but Shishakly's best estimate is that the camp now is now home to some 26,000 internally displaced persons.

Mayada reciting the Qur'an

'So... do you think this camp is a place where people are planning to stay?' Shishakly asks. We are on the road back to Reyhanlı. Before I can begin to fail to answer the unanswerable question, his phone rings, for the millionth time that day. No-one has done more than Shishakly to ensure that the camp is a place that its inhabitants can imagine staying in. He is not entirely alone: the Turkish Red Crescent provided the initial tents, and still provides a meagre breakfast. However, the major aid NGOs and the UN have been unable to provide any aid across the border.

And is a camp like this ever a place to imagine staying in for long? In the encroaching darkness, below a Turkish military base on the hill opposite, a child, his leg amputated at the thigh, hobbles on crutches to the camp gates, surrounded, thankfully, by friends. 'Why does he sound like us?' the grandmothers sitting in the mud enquire of my Syrian guide, asking about my Arabic. I say I lived in Gaza and they smile big smiles—those big smiles, the same ones as in Gaza—and they say, almost triumphantly: 'Ah, yes! What happened to you is now happening to us!' Gaza may be a perennial symbol of perennially-manufactured humanitarian crisis—but the sheer scale of the Syrian crisis clearly dwarfs it: references to the Palestinian *nakba* (catastrophe) abound in conversation.

Hassan attends the Salam School for Refugees in Reyhaniyeh, Turkey, just across the border from Atmeh

Night falls on Atmeh and brings with it a biting cold wind, and I am the only one wearing a decent coat. The sounds of the camp's teenagers' football game dry up: a real football field, indestructible footballs and trainers are on the Maram Foundation's list of priorities. Mahmoud, a teenager, asks: 'How is it inside?' 'Inside' means, for once, inside Turkey: not further inside Syria. '*Akeed sa'abeh*,' (surely it's difficult) he affirms. 'What do they have there? Here we have everything'. Of course nothing could be further from the truth—unless, of course, 'everything' is the felt dignity of remaining in one's own country—unlike the millions of refugees in Turkey, Jordan, Lebanon, Iraq and beyond.

Back in Reyhanlı the ambulances run up and down the main street—inevitably called Ataturk, ferrying the wounded from the air strikes just over the hills. It's rare to hear them in Reyhanlı itself: the distinct, stunning-but-muffled sound of shelling nearby prompts all-day 'did you hear it?', including on the part of the Syrians. Half the cars in the streets have Aleppo or Idlib number plates: those of the 'lucky' ones who got away.

The Revolution House School, Atmeh Camp, Syria

Since March 2013, Atmeh camp's size has stabilised at some 30,000. By February 2014, the Return School is no more. It has been replaced by a few mud-floor, unheated rooms and now dubbed the School of Wisdom. There are two other schools: the Revolution House, and another run by Salafi Islamists on an Islamic curriculum. The village of Atmeh, some eight kilometres away, is under the control of ISIS (the Islamic State in Iraq and Syria) militias. The latest photo update from the camp's Facebook page is of 'School Street'. It shows the same river of mud that the alleyway was eight months ago.

The work of Maram and others is irreplaceable. But it is implausible that camp institutions run by volunteers on donations would ever be able to meet the most minimal humanitarian needs of the camp's population—much less to ensure their human rights, including the right to education. Without a stable ceasefire or humanitarian corridors from Damascus, the only short-term solution is aid via the Turkish border. As Human Rights Watch noted ahead of the most recent donor pledging conference, 'the human cost of this crisis has been increased exponentially by Syria's policy of deliberately obstructing aid'. While Syria has permitted some movement of aid from neighbouring Iraq, Jordan, and Lebanon, it has steadfastly refused to allow aid from Turkey to reach those in need in northern Syria. Despite a non-binding UN Security Council Presidential Statement from October 2013 calling for access 'including across conflict lines and where appropriate, across borders from neighbouring countries', no solution for those in Atmeh is in sight.

The number of people displaced by the conflict in Syria is unimaginable. Mid-2013 UNHCR figures cite 4.3 million internally displaced persons to add to the two million refugees outside, not including the millions more within Syria in need of humanitarian assistance. Effects on the right to education are especially cruel: a year ago already, '2,362 of Syria's 22,000 school buildings—more than 10 per cent of Syria's schools—had sustained damage as a result of the conflict, and 1,468 additional schools could no longer be used for education because they had become shelters for internally displaced persons.'

The Syrian conflict is many things, including the gravest displacement and humanitarian crisis of the century. Above all, in the long-term, it is a crisis of children's rights and education. According to the UNHCR, of the 2.4 million refugees registered by January 2014, over a million are children. According to UNICEF, about 865,000 of the refugees are children, and 70% of them are not enrolled in school. The many more internally displaced children are worse off still.

Fears of an entire lost generation of Syrian children can hardly be overstated. The key short-term question is how best to address the loss of up to three years of primary education. As great a challenge is how to avoid the decades-long catastrophic impact on future Syrian society of the loss of secondary (and university) education when the skills from these will be crucial to rebuilding. By way of example, 'the UNHCR estimates that 20 per cent of Syrian refugee children drop out of school in Lebanon—the biggest problem being among children over twelve', with fears they will lose 'the spirit of education' even if provided with opportunities to return. Field workers in Lebanon note 'it can be particularly difficult for children older than twelve to attend school—some have been out of the system for too long, feel too old to re-enter, or have been working and believe that this is a better use of their time.' Attention to the needs of refugee university students is scarcely less urgent. In a crisis, comprehensive, short and medium-term solutions cannot obscure planning for long-term needs. One can only hope this will restore to Hania in Atmeh her right to education, before it is too late.

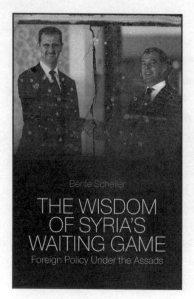

THE WISDOM OF SYRIA'S WAITING GAME

Foreign Policy Under the Assads

Bente Scheller

Syrian foreign policy, always opaque, has become an even greater puzzle during the Syrian revolt. Irrespective of the regime's international isolation in the wake of its violent response to domestic protest, it has paid lip-service to international peace plans while unperturbedly crushing the rebellion. The rare televised appearances of President Assad have shown a leader detached from reality. Has he—in his own words—'gone crazy'? In this book long-time Syria analyst and former diplomat Bente Scheller contends that Bashar Assad's deadly waiting game is following its own logic: whatever difficulties the Syrian regime has faced, its previous experience has been that it can simply sit out the current crisis.

ISBN: 9781849042864
£30.00 / Hardback / 244pp

The difference this time is that Syria faces a double crisis—internal and external. While Hafez Assad, renowned as an astute politician, adapted to new challenges, his son, Bashar, seems to have no alternative plan of action.

Scheller's timely book analyses Syrian foreign policy after the global upheavals of 1989, which was at the time a glorious new beginning for the regime. She shows how Bashar Assad, by ignoring change both inside Syria and in the region, has sacrificed his father's focus on national security in favour of a policy of regime survival and offers a candid analysis of the successes and shortcomings of Syrian foreign policy in recent years.

'Bente Scheller has written a timely and sober analysis of Syrian foreign policy. Anyone interested in understanding why the Assads have lasted for over 40 years and why their missteps led to the revolt of 2011 should read this book.' — Joshua M. Landis, Director, Center for Middle East Studies, University of Oklahoma, and author of SyriaComment.com

WWW.HURSTPUBLISHERS.COM/BOOK/THE-WISDOM-OF-SYRIAS-WAITING-GAME

41 GREAT RUSSELL ST, LONDON WC1B 3PL
WWW.HURSTPUBLISHERS.COM
WWW.FBOOK.COM/HURSTPUBLISHERS
020 7255 2201

FIVE STORIES

Zakaria Tamer

The Speakers

When I miaow like a cat, my mother and my father make fun of me, they say that there are two cats in the house now, a female and a male. My brother, who is ten years older than I am, and who always brags about studying French at school, makes fun of me too, but I don't react to their teasing. I just smile, because they don't understand that I only meow when I want to talk about something with my white cat, whose language I understand. I also understand the walls' language, and the trees' language, and the birds'.

Cats don't utter a word until they've thought about it for a long time.

Walls are talkative; if you ask them a question, they'll go on for hours looking for an answer.

Trees prefer silence, and they claim that words tire them out and make them forget their work.

Different kinds of birds have different characters. Crows only speak when the question asked sparks their curiosity; doves like gentle, tranquil words, all the nightingale's words are songs, and the migratory sparrows talk even faster than their speed while flying from branch to branch.

A few days ago, the wall informed me that my brother had got hold of a magazine full of photos of naked women, and that he had hidden it under his bed. The wall hadn't lied to me, because I found the magazine under the bed, and I looked through it. Then the wall asked me what I thought of what I'd seen, and I said that my brother had bought the magazine and paid money to see what I see for free when I go with my mother to the hammam in the souk. Then I showed the photos in the magazine to my cat, and she yawned and said: I'd rather have some meat to eat.

I asked the crow about the difference between men and women. He thought about it, then he said to me: 'Women are afraid of crows, and men aren't.'

I didn't put the magazine back under my brother's bed. I hid it under my own bed. For several days my brother kept looking at my mother, ashamed and confused. He obeyed all her orders, because he thought she was the one who had found the magazine under his bed and had taken it. My brother didn't get his magazine back until he gave me his blue rubber ball that I had been longing to have.

I saw my mother deep in conversation with three neighbour women, and I went up to them and asked her what was the difference between a man and a woman. The neighbours laughed, and one of them said: 'Mashallah ! All he has to do now is ask what the bridegroom does on the wedding night!'

So I asked my mother and the neighbour women: 'What does the bridegroom do on the wedding night?'

The neighbour women laughed even harder, and my mother ordered me to be quiet and not to interrupt grown-ups when they were talking among themselves, and to go away and play with my ball.

I was angry, and I threw the ball as hard as I could and as far as I could. The ball flew up and didn't come back down. I couldn't find it, even though I knocked on the doors of all the houses in the neighbourhood.

After a while, I was sure that a crow, who didn't answer me when I spoke to him, was the one who had taken the ball when it flew up, and given it to his own son.

When I told my mother what had happened she smiled, and said to me 'Little crows have the right to play ball too!'

But I didn't agree with her, and I kept on throwing stones at the crows and making them caw with rage.

The Trap

My brother went into the guest room. I tried to follow him, but he quickly shut and locked the door behind him. Then I tried to look in the window, but he rushed over and lowered the blinds. I ran to the keyhole and tried to look through it, but my brother blew snuff powder through it into my face and I began to sneeze and sneeze, till tears ran down my cheeks.

My mother, who was cutting up vegetables in the kitchen, asked me what was the matter. I told her what my brother had done, and she laughed. Then she advised me to stop being so curious and stop meddling in what was none of my business.

But my mother hadn't noticed my cat who was coming closer to the platter of meat that was to be cooked with the vegetables, and she ate it all.

When my mother had finished cutting up the vegetables, she looked in surprise at the empty meat platter and she exclaimed: 'Where is the meat?'

I said: 'The cat ate it!'

She said: 'But why didn't you stop her, and why didn't you tell me?'

I said: 'I only interfere in what's my business, and I have nothing to do with what goes on in the kitchen!'

My mother cooked the vegetables with no meat at all, and I ate them grudgingly.

But my mother wasn't angry when she caught me a few days later listening in on my grandfather who was talking to my grandmother about his will and what was in it; she whispered to me insisting that I tell her what I had heard.

The Postponed Gift

My grandfather coughed a lot. He drank a big glass of water that my grandmother gave him, then he said to her that his health was not good and that it was high time he made his will, so no one would suffer any injustice.

My grandmother said to him: 'You're wrong to think about such things, we only have one son and the poor boy does everything he can to please us.'

My grandfather said: 'And you? What will become of you when I'm gone?'

She answered, laughing, 'No one lives very long in my family. I'll die before you do, and I won't need anyone but you.'

Then my grandfather saw that I was there listening to them. He called me over, and he said: 'Listen, grandson, your grandfather has neglected you, and he'd like to give you a gift that's worth something, but he doesn't know what would please you.'

I said to my grandfather: 'Buy me a dog!'

My grandmother said: 'Don't you know that dogs detest cats, and cats detest dogs, for as long as we can remember?'

And my grandfather said: 'The dog would fight with your cat, and he might even kill her.'

I said to my grandfather: 'Then buy me a horse. I love horses.'

My grandmother said: 'And what kind of love is that? Do you let everyone who loves you climb on your back?'

And my grandfather said to me: 'Where is this horse going to sleep? In your room? A horse needs a stable.'

I said to my grandfather: 'Buy me a little television set. I'll put it in my room, next to my bed.'

My grandfather said: 'Watching television will keep you from sleeping. You're still little, you need to sleep a lot to grow.'

I said to my grandfather: 'Buy me a bicycle'.

My grandmother said: 'God forbid! You'll fall off and break your neck!'

My grandfather said: 'You might be run over by a car and we'd be reading the Fatiha for your soul!'

I stopped talking, puzzled, and my grandfather looked at me attentively, and said to me: 'The best gift for you is a comb to comb your hair. It's always tangled.'

I looked at my grandfather, who had no more hair, and I said to him: 'I'm the one who'll buy a comb for you, that will please you!'

My grandmother laughed, and my grandfather knit his brows and frowned, which was not a good sign, and I didn't get a dog who would have barked at anyone who bothered me, or a horse I'd have climbed on to gallop together in the park, or a television to amuse me, or a bicycle that would have made all the boys in the neighbourhood jealous, or a comb to comb my hair that is still always tangled.

Rose or Onion?

When my mother saw me, I was standing in front of the mirror with a cigarette between my lips. She pulled it out of my mouth angrily, and said to me in a tone of reproach: 'You're no bigger than a cigarette and you're smoking? The cigarette is taller than you are!'

I said: 'Look at me! I'm much bigger than the cigarette!'

She said: 'Who gave you that cigarette? Don't lie!'

I said: 'I took it out of Papa's pack of cigarettes.'

She said: 'You only took one?'

I said: 'Only one.'

She said: 'Don't lie!'

I said: 'I'm not lying! Search me!'

She said: 'And when did you take it?'

I said: 'Last night, after dinner.'

And my mother spoke to me in a wise, gentle voice, and put my head on her lap, and I fell asleep.

That evening, when my father came home from work and we were seated around the table as usual for dinner, my mother told him what I had done. My brother laughed, and he whispered in my ear, pleased with himself, that I was going to get a good spanking, and advised me to get ready for it or run away. I looked at my father fearfully, but he stroked my hair and said to my mother: 'You can see that this little monkey is his father's son. When I smoked for the first time, I was even smaller than he is.'

My mother was angry and shouted: 'Is that what a father tells his sons? He'll corrupt them, and ruin all the care I take in raising them!'

My father said to my mother, all the while eating his dinner with gusto: 'Sweetheart! Don't make a drama out of something unimportant! The little rose grows into a big rose, and the little onion grows into a big onion. The onion won't turn into a rose, or the rose into an onion.'

My mother's face turned very red, and she said to my father threateningly: 'If you don't stop talking like that I'm going to scream and run out of the house barefoot!'

I said to my mother: 'If you scream the whole neighbourhood will think someone died at our house.'

She said: 'I'll tell them you died and I'm well rid of you!'

I said: 'And if you walk around outdoors barefoot you'll hurt your feet.'

My mother said to me angrily: 'Shut up!'

I looked at my father, perplexed, and was about to say something when he said: 'Are you deaf? Didn't you hear what your mother said? Be quiet and eat!'

I didn't say a single word all evening, and I didn't answer when anyone asked me a question. I stayed silent, I stayed mute, and I remained silent the next day. Not a single word emerged from my mouth all day long, and all my mother's efforts didn't succeed in making me utter one. But I had warned my cat, the wall, the trees and the birds that I was on strike against words, and this did not sadden them, they didn't blame me. They considered that this was a day of rest for them that they had been waiting for a long time. So I got angry with them, and I began to accuse them and insult them out loud. My mother came rushing over and she said to me: 'What's going on? I see you've found your tongue! Who were you insulting? How many times have I told you not to insult people?'

I said: 'I wasn't insulting anyone, I was insulting myself because I made you angry last night.'

She hugged me tenderly, then she went off and came back with a little camera.

She said that during his last visit, my grandfather had asked for a new photo of me. She had me stand in a sunny spot facing the camera, and she put a cigarette between my lips. She took the photo with the cigarette hanging from the corner of my mouth and she said to me, smiling, 'I know your grandfather, he'll like this picture and it will make him laugh.'

Then my mother took another photo where I was holding my father's dagger. I had my right hand raised as if I was about to attack someone. But my grandfather never got the two photos, because my mother didn't know how to focus the camera – in the first photo, I was a headless body, and in the second you saw only my hand holding the dagger with its curved blade.

The Gazelle-Eaters

During the week of his school exams, my brother abandoned his usual haughtiness, and became polite, modest and timid. He promised me that if he passed his exams, he would give me a book with coloured pictures of gazelles.

I said: 'You'll pass, and you'll forget to give me the book.'

But he swore that he would keep his promise.

My brother knew how much I loved gazelles, since I had seen a gazelle in the market, tied to the door of the shop that sells live chickens. I asked my mother about her, and she said the gazelle was there to be sold. I said: 'And what will the person who buys her do with her?'

My mother said: 'He'll cut her throat, skin her, and prepare the meat to be cooked and eaten.'

The gazelle standing in front of the shop door was beautiful. I had never seen a creature so calm: she moved slowly and looked at what was around her with sorrowful eyes. She touched my heart and never left it. At home, I got into the habit of watching my brother, and every time he laughed and was in a good mood, I asked him questions about gazelles. He spoke to me about them and I listened to him attentively and respectfully as if I were at the mosque.

'Gazelles live in the desert... Gazelles only eat plants... The gazelle harms no one... Gazelles don't go to school... You never see a gazelle going for a ride in a car... A gazelle walks on its four hooves as long as it lives...'

I asked my brother: 'How do people hunt them?'

My brother said to me: 'Gazelles are not strong, they have no weapons to conquer humans, so as soon as they see them, they escape, and they can run as fast as the wind.'

I asked my brother: 'Can the wind run?'

My brother said angrily: 'If you keep on asking me stupid questions, I won't tell you anything else.'

But I begged him: 'Don't stop talking. I won't say anything else.'

My brother went on telling me about gazelles.

'Gazelles run so swiftly that they used to be able to escape from humans. But people invented a car that's faster than the gazelle, and now they can catch them easily.'

I frowned and asked my brother angrily: 'And who invented the car?'

My brother answered laughing: 'As for me, praise God, I didn't invent the car or the aeroplane or the tank!'

The day that the exam results were announced, my brother came home from school jumping with joy, for he had seen his name on the list of those who had passed with honours. I said to him: 'And where's the book you promised me?'

'What book?', said my brother.

I said: 'The book with pictures of gazelles.'

My brother said: 'I'll buy it for you tomorrow.'

I said: 'Why don't you buy it today?'

My brother answered, laughing: 'Not only do you act like a beggar, you've got conditions!'

My brother kept his promise, but he didn't buy me the book, he gave me a little ceramic statuette of a gazelle. He claimed all the copies of the book with pictures of gazelles had disappeared. But I wasn't angry. I was happy that gazelles had friends that wanted to know about them. I liked the statuette of the gazelle, and I got into the habit of sitting down next to it every day for hours. I'd look at it and ask it many questions, but it didn't answer me with words, as if it were deaf.

But one day I was playing ball in my room and the ball hit the gazelle statuette and it fell on the floor. It broke into little pieces as if a car had run over it.

I was so sad that my brother promised he would give me a live gazelle.

My grandfather and grandmother invited us to lunch. While we were eating the rice, the meat and the vegetables, my father, my mother and my brother complimented my grandmother on her cooking, and I said that the meat was delicious, I had never eaten anything so good. My grandfather laughed and said that my grandmother was famous for her recipe for gazelle. My brother opened his eyes wide and stared at me uneasily, but I pretended not to care and kept on eating as if I hadn't heard.

From *The Hedgehog*, translated from the Arabic by Marilyn Hacker

POEMS

Golan Haji

The Box Of Pain

I support you, who are weak like me,
not as two hands support the chins of sages
not as a disabled man holds up another
not as a cane with which the blind stab
leaves fallen onto narrow pavements
not as a ball on which clowns balance
as if it were one more last planet
rolling over this mad one.

I'm far away but brace you in your solitude
as an index finger rises past a widow's cheek
wobbling like an arrow just as it's being shot
and on its tip a crystal of salt glimmers
returning to the eye that shed it
submerged in shadows & wings.

*** **** ***

If the dead were buried
how would pain be ?
What is the point of cursing the curse ?

Life is loss.

And this silence the most heavy.
How slow words are
flowing & becoming rusted in the blood of night
or rising up like sap to the dusty leaves.

The branches are brawling & shaking
but there is no wind.

Right now, as lonely as you,
as our mother, as this tree,
another bird has fluttered up that we didn't see.
The house of screaming is jagged out
a diamond cracking the world's grimy pane.

*** **** ***

This daybreak you weren't there,
when patients, passengers & soldiers
with bald or shaven heads
loomed out like far-off windows from dark huts.
There was a hazy mist which didn't last that
the boy crossed in front of the hospital gate
where he found a pistol in the grass.
You were not there.

Now you're a story being told in a place you're not.
Your throat, that box of pain,
is full of bones & feathers.
In the white of your eye
there's a blood spot, small & rusted,
like a sun setting in the distance
over a snow field
trampled down by straggles of hungry soldiers.

from 'March Light'

I hide my hell inside me while I smile: that's my act as an actor, all the
time & even when alone.

If I really killed everything I would be alone & dead: when I was being
inattentive I did indeed kill everything & then I killed myself. And now
I hate what I secretly remember & I yearn for what terrifies me. Back
then I was fond of the last sip of life in a dying mouth & I was saying: my
terror breathes in the same air as your laughter; but I myself wasn't the

one who stumbled over your shadows, to pounce on myself like a rabid dog.

What I know of the guillotine is just its name, whenever I heard it I saw the beautiful head of Marie Antoinette & the dangerous oratory of Robespierre & a cigarette in the corner of Albert Camus' mouth. I remember how Dostoyevsky contemplated the ideas that might occur to a severed head during the very few moments when it was seeing its body departing forever, the distracted glance of its terrified eye & blood flooding the block of the guillotine like a sacrifice for justice & 'its long procession of punishments'. But I don't know what this guillotine is that has terrified so many people simply by its name, just as I don't know what it is that is horrifying me.

What I know will always remain little, little & useless.

Whenever I took a ticket I saw myself dead in an accident, and in every piece of meat I chew I'm eating some human being I don't know who.

My eyes move as if they were reading a continuous warning that is neither seen nor could easily disappear: Do not say this word. Do not ask for forgiveness. Do not prolong any apology.

Then my eyelids close as if it were the final closure of the eyes of a severed head.

I know that the tired are called by the roofs of towers to give their bodies as a gift to the fence spears

 & that highways insist they throw themselves beneath car wheels

& that the cleanliness of the pharmacies with their neon hits seduces them to steal what will hypnotise them forever

But I disappeared from my own memory, or maybe I vanished & remember no-one.

And because of my excessive silence, everything I think of is erasing me: I am everyone with whom I've talked.

In this huge stillness no idea is my own any more, here where I recall

no name that hasn't terrified me & don't remember anyone to whom I
didn't apologise, I called those I thought of as friends & invited them to
an empty house in order to ensure they'd understand this joke I could
never tell well & so experience my absence.

Then how beautiful their sighs were & how real & true.

*** **** ***

The sparrow that flew down from the washing-line recognized me
without knowing my name. His legs were thinner than the line, weak
but they served his needs well. I terrified him when I appeared & the
terror took his wings high & away. He doesn't differentiate between all
of us who are called human; it's the same whether it's me or someone
else since his shining eyes don't feel safe with any of us. But I hate it that
I keep watch over the name I was given to capture me, that I drag it & it
drags me, and that it's stuck to my face & has become part of my voice.
Sometimes it seems strange to me when I read it or hear it, or it bores
me & I detest it. Like everyone I have spent a long time imprisoning
myself in my name, since all of us are buried alive, each in his own : a
grave of fear & delight & misunderstanding.

(translated by Stephen Watts and the author)

FACING EAST

Ruth Padel

This steel shell memorial to two lives,
a composer and his singer, looms at me
before sun-up like a guardian of the earth -
or a freezing North Sea re-run of the birth
of Aphrodite. *Dark,* says the sculptor
in her book. *Dark like a wave born
backwards, shattering as it breaks.
Light and dark like life and death,
part shining and part rust, with movement
between colours as between the forms.*
I creep in and run my hand along a frilled
bronze rim. A bivalve - two shells or
a single broken one self-joining at the core.
I think of the philandering sigh of ocean,
life-long partners betraying and forgiving
and Plato's cave: the fire, the sun

and how, arguing against his gift, he banned
artists for reflecting our world back
with a false beauty, making real unreal,
enticing us to take the shadow for the thing.
I gaze out, invisible as Echo,
at a lead gauze sea. Over my head
the breaker's cusp is a fanned-card silhouette.
Round the edge, letters punched out of metal
like finger-holes in a flute, write in paling sky,
I hear the voices of the drowned. Iron cloud
on the horizon splices day from night
like west from east. On the news
is flat-to-flat urban warfare in Aleppo
and air attacks on Gaza. Over here, in kitchens,

at the Tuesday evening pub quiz, on the bus or tube,
how quickly arguments flare up

even in England; even if we've never been
to what we call the middle of the east.
We identify. Some chasm through the centre
must be in and of us all: creatures of relation
and division, always wrong-footed by the past
on its bed of ice, the sub-tectonic clash
of ancient histories on common ground.
Suddenly I see this rifted arabesque,
a monument to music joined only at its core,
is all of us. *Harmonia's* gift is cursed.
She can't help it, she's Aphrodite's child –
one false note and what you get is discord –
and her father, lord of war,
is Apollo's enemy. East or west, the first thing
looting soldiers smash (before starting on God's
perfect instrument, the larynx) is an oud or violin.

Sing the sadness and pain of *Sabah,*
the microtonal range of the *maqam.*
Hijaz, conjuring distant desert
and our longing for it. Sing the body:
tongue and teeth to whistle through,
palms to clap, lips to hum, vibrate
or tremble – and the fragile, mucus-laden
vox humana. Sing also of David's harp
placed sideways on the mountain, pitched
to catch wind blowing from rocks
below the tower of Lebanon which looks
toward the oldest city in the world
whose sky burns indigo, dark-pearled
as strong espresso, above the fountain
in Umayyad Mosque. Where children

used to lick pistachio-starred ice cream
of orchid root from *Bakdash Parlour*,
and now play Asking-for-Papers-of-Identity-

at-Gun-Point. Where Saladin and the head
of John the Baptist both lie buried. Where old men
with pewter urns poured tamarisk-flavour
liquorice in jumps the way a flat stone
skims water. Al Fayha, Fragrant City, home
to *rosa damascena* and the damask plum:
these newly dawn-lit pebbles of the west
glow like your own spell-bound *intarsia*
whose weavers set compound
floats of warp and weft at angles to reflect
light scatter-wise depending who you are
and where you're looking from.
What will survive are meanings we have found

in what the world has made. Pattern
is how we see: as in those burnished steps –
infused with cardamom, I remember –
in the run-up to Al-Hamidiyah Souq
beside the citadel. And at the top, strings
of hanging flip-flops, rosewood sets
of backgammon like puzzle books
inlaid with mother-of-pearl, glinting
gargoyle fish and stalls of samite
whose glitter-twill depends
on optic interference like the play of light
in Damascus Twist: the mystery metal
welded in carbon fire, which can cut a rifle
barrel, or a hair floating across a dagger;
the iron-plait steel whose laminate spirals,
acid-bitten into waves, resemble damask.

What would we be without desire for form?
We look for omens in a flock of redwing,
the gods' will in dappled entrails, outline
of a consoling story in the stars. We break the line
to shape it, string catgut over membrane,
set a ten-foot memorial to music –
a scallop shell, a pilgrim's prayer –
in shale of an eroding coast

and turn it east to face the storm.
Voices of the drowned. I watch dawn
gild the sea to iridescence. Sea-birds arc
and squawk and flicker-print the air.
Breakers roar on draining shingle.
Palmetto patterns dint the waves
from grey to silver, hyacinth and jade.
Making is our defence against the dark.

POEMS

Moniza Alvi

Little god, your sun sleeps
beneath the eyelid of the day.

Intent on waking it
the twin dogs
of the past and future
rush in from the heathland,
can't stop leaping up.

No one can restrain them –
their enthusiasm, their ferocity.

Little god, a wordless word
could raise the eyelid of the day.

*** **** ***

After the nightmare, little god
(three times I was immersed in it –
slept and woke and slept and woke
and slept again) here you are,

but further off and quivering

like the high leaves on a tall tree.
Could you have threaded into it
that silver, hopeful strand:
'This isn't really happening'?

The dread of being ill-prepared.
The horror of inspection.
                         Little god,
like me, in fact, you don't give up –
beak-like you tear
at the ligaments of the dream

*** **** ***

Little god, in the frostfire of an iris
in the gunshot of a pupil
in an eye behind an eye
a miniature world is spinning.

What news from it?
What makes it turn and turn again
far far away?
An unexpected thing
like memory with its thirst for detail.

From *Little God, What News?*

REVIEWS

WHERE NOW?

Laurens de Rooij

The situation in Syria has reached the same stage as the killings in Bosnia and Rwanda. As the fighting rages the list of war crimes and the death toll continue to rise. While the conflict has its origins in domestic politics, it involves a string of actors and has become very complex. It is clear that, with the current imbalance of power, neither the fragmented opposition nor the Assad regime can win the conflict outright. The array of competing interests and contending perspectives make it difficult to imagine a viable political solution that would be acceptable to all interested parties. As UN Secretary General Ban Ki-moon puts it, 'the UN, the US, the European Union and the countries of the Middle East are flummoxed on how to end the conflict'.

The Syria Dilemma is a collection of twenty-one essays that attempt to critically engage with the complexities of the situation and suggest possible arguments for humanitarian, military and political interventions. The contributors highlight the fragmentation and intricacies of the Syrian conflict, with some specialists warning that the worst is still to come. If there is a common theme in the essays, it is 'the responsibility to protect' the Syrian population, which ought to be, it is suggested, the guiding principle of any intervention. In contrast, *Revolt in Syria* focuses on the story of the country's 'silent' civilian population. 'The international narrative on the revolt in Syria has been decidedly one-sided', Starr points out. Western reports utilise a narrative that suggests that the spread of the 'Arab Spring' from North Africa to Syria has divided the country into pro-regime militants from the Alawite sect of President Bashar al-Assad or fellow Shia sympathisers and the Sunni rebels described as the 'Free Syrian Army'. But the reality is not black and white. Not all Syrians desire the removal of the regime. Neither are all Alawites on the side of the regime. There are Sunnis who will die for Assad just as there are Alawites who have joined the Free Syrian Army. Those who support the Assad regime may do so because of fear or pragmatic reasons, and this support may change once they have a free choice. And not all opponents of the regime wish to see a democratic Syria. Starr offers anecdotes and an analysis based on interviews and fieldwork that exposes a reality that is far more complex.

The origins of the Syrian conflict, Starr points out, lay not in sectarianism but in historically rooted resentment against the regime. The opposition drew its early strength from the rural areas that were severely affected by the 2008–9 droughts. The regime's policies disproportionately affected the land holdings of the Sunni population and the traditional merchants in places like Hama and Homs, which became the strongholds of the rebellion. The ruthless response of the regime to early demonstrations left the disenchanted population with little choice. They had no option, 'whether they wanted or not', but 'to pick sides'. Moreover, it was clear that 'those in power will fight to the last man' and 'will not negotiate', given that 'the concept is alien to them in their everyday lives'. Once the conflict accelerated, the regime used the spectre of sectarianism to discredit the uprising. The arrival of foreign jihadis provided them with extra ammunition.

So what should be done about the conflict in Syria? What are the ethical and political dilemmas in the debate?

The potential solutions to the Syrian crisis, political, humanitarian or military, are overshadowed by the history of recent interventions in Iraq, Afghanistan and Libya. As Fareed Zakaria argues, the 2003 US invasion of Iraq is a cautionary tale about the risks of military intervention. Shadi Hamid suggests that 'the war, itself, was one of the greatest strategic blunders in the recent history of American foreign policy. But its legacy is proving just as damaging'. This damage is evident in both the lack of military support for the opposition as well as the inability of the West to take military action against Assad. The involvement of jihadi movements in the Syrian conflict has added an extra layer of complexity. Jihadist veterans of the Iraqi army that the United States dissolved have taken up arms not only against the Shia dominated government in Iraq but also against the Syrian regime, leading to a paralysis of Western strategy. (Meanwhile, Iranian-backed Iraqi Shia militias are formed under the nose of the Malki government, and then sent to fight on Assad's front lines). The international community, says Thomas Pierret, cannot conceive, decide or agree on a suitable approach that will either deter or aid Islamist extremists. So even if Western and regional powers would like to remove the Assad regime and isolate Iran, direct military intervention had to be ruled out (although precautionary measures were taken, such as placing NATO Patriot missiles in Turkey). The overall emphasis has been on humanitarian intervention, and even that has been limited. Thus, we are faced with an ethical question: when does the so-called humanitarian intervention turn into the responsibility to protect the massacre of innocent civilians?

Revolt in Syria, Stephen Starr (Hurst, London, 2012)
The Syria Dilemma, Nader Hashemi & Danny Postel (eds) (MIT Press, London & Cambridge, MA 2013)

In a speech to the United Nations on 24 September 2013, US President Barack Obama declared: 'Some may disagree, but I believe that America is exceptional, in part because we have shown a willingness through the sacrifice of blood and treasure to stand up not only for our own narrow self-interests, but for the interests of all'. In the Syrian context, this rhetoric has been exposed as shallow. The military interventions in Iraq and Afghanistan were clearly (perceived to be) in the interest of America. The intervention in Libya had both humanitarian as well as strategic interests for Britain and France. But there are no clear cut Western interests in Syria and the 'all' in 'the interests of all' clearly does not include the innocent civilians being massacred on a daily basis. So the need to stop the bloodshed in Syria only receives lip service.

The main argument againt military intervention is clearly stated by Asli Bâli and Aziz Rana. 'There is likely no form of direct or indirect military involvement in the conflict', they write, 'that will spare civilians or advance either side towards a decisive victory – there are too many interveners and too many strategic interests at stake'. Arming the rebels is also seen as counterproductive. Although weight of numbers on the rebel side means that whenever serious supplies do go to the rebels, they make immediate progress on the ground, Marc Lynch notes 'it's difficult to produce a single example in modern history of a strategy of arming rebels actually succeeding'. The ethical problems then revolve around whether you allow Assad to massacre his people or whether you kill innocent people to stop

Assad from killing, or whether you arm the rebels and perhaps exacerbate violence and suffering.

This leaves us with diplomacy. But there is little joy here either. Christopher R. Hill tell us that it is not the United States' reluctance on military intervention that is at the heart of the issue but rather 'the administration's unwillingness to lead a sustained and substantial diplomatic effort to identify political arrangements that could offer Syrians a way out of civil war'. The problem, however, is not limited to US diplomacy; the framework of international diplomacy itself constitutes a problem: 'the failure to take diplomacy seriously underscores a profound moral hazard generated by the international community's prevailing framework'. So we are left in limbo: neither a military nor a diplomatic solution seems possible.

At the heart of the diplomatic issue is the role of regional powers. Although historically Iraq served as a strategic partner for the US in the region (to counter Iranian influence), 'liberated' Iraq is a staunch ally of Iran, which along with Russia is now aiding the Syrian regime. In turn Syria has become a key battleground for Saudi Arabia and Iran competing with each other for regional hegemony.

With military intervention ruled out and diplomatic efforts thwarted, what other options are there? The contributors to *The Syria Dilemma* suggest no-kill zones, no-fly zones, safe zones, drone attacks, sanctions, and large-scale humanitarian relief.

But the most original suggestion comes from Christopher Hill who points to the war in Bosnia as a possible model for resolving the Syrian conflict. The endgame strategy for Bosnia involved recognition of Bosnia's sovereignty and territorial integrity within its existing borders, division of Bosnia into two entities, a Bosnian Serb entity and a Muslim-Croat federation and the possibility of conducting a future referendum on secession. To persuade the two sides to accept this deal, the strategy also involved placing American military troops in the service of the diplomatic effort. In presenting the parties with the outlines of a possible diplomatic deal, the Unites States made clear what price each side would have to pay if negotiations failed. On this model, the endgame strategy for Syria would then be the recognition of rebel territory as a sovereign area with territorial integrity within its existing borders, possibly arranged in a fashion similar to Aceh in Indonesia or the regionalised political system in Belgium. Syria would be divided into multiple entities, each given the opportunity to hold a referendum on secession and become an independent state. To persuade the two sides to accept this deal, the strategy would entail placing troops on the ground to support the diplomatic effort. The international community would lift the arms embargo, provide arms and training to rebel forces, and conduct air strikes for a transition period in order to enable the rebels to take control of and defend the proportion of territory allocated to them under the peace plan. Conversely, if the rebels rejected an agreement the international community would adopt a policy of 'lift and leave', lifting the arms embargo but otherwise leaving the rebels to their own devices. However, it is difficult to imagine that balkanisation of Syria would be a popular solution; or, indeed, it would be acceptable to any of the participants in the conflict. Indeed, this solution would necessitate the ethnic cleansing of the Sunni majority from the coastal area, and would leave most of Syria without access to the sea.

Both *The Syria Dilemma* and *Revolt in Syria* point towards three potential outcomes for the conflict: a regionalised conflict, a contained civil war and a negotiated settlement.

Starr reports that most Syrians are aware of the potential regional (and global) implications of a Syrian state collapse. Syria, he writes, is 'the key stone right in the middle' of the Middle East arch. The conflict has the potential to set the whole Middle East on fire. Already, Iran, Hezbollah, Saudi Arabia and Qatar are actively involved, Lebanon is slipping steadily back into war, and car bombs explode in southern Turkey.

In the 'contained civil war' scenario, the conflict rages on, neither side has an upper hand, but bloodshed continues and refugees multiply. External powers aid their favoured players with military support but do not break the cycle of violence. Syria bleeds to death slowly but surely. The overall interests of external powers seem best served by attempting to contain the conflict within Syria's borders.

The third scenario, that of a negotiated settlement on the lines of the Bosnian model suggested by Christopher Hill, would lead to either the internal fragmentation of Syria or a transitional period of ceasefire that enables the breaking down and removal of the Assad regime. But as Starr points out, a total dissolution or destruction of state institutions would leave the country at the mercy of antagonistic groups within the opposition, and everything would have to be rebuilt. Syria's Kurdish community has pushed Assad forces from Kurdish-majority areas, but is wary of the Syrian Arab opposition, particularly the Islamist forces. It is not clear what role the Kurds would be willing to play in rebuilding Syria. An Islamist takeover in a post-Assad Syria devoid of basic institutions is also a real possibility. Moreover, a fragmented Syria would also be exposed to existential threats.

Not surprisingly, the internal fragmentation of Syria is loathed by rebel groups. The Syrian people, as Stephen Zunes notes, 'do not want to choose between savage and coercive forces'; neither do they wish to see their country balkanised. It is up to the international community to make sure that these are not the only options the Syrian people are left with when all is said and done. The opposition too must prepare for a transitional period by uniting and producing an agenda for governing Syria that emphasises respect for human rights, tolerance of dissent, and democracy. 'A stronger, respected civilian governance structure would have more authority to negotiate an orderly transition in lieu of the chaos and endless civil war that many dread', writes Kenneth Roth. It can also help hold off the fears that a successor or new government might be worse than the current regime.

In many respects *The Syria Dilemma* is a pretty depressing book. There is wide disagreement over what can and ought to be done amongst the contributors, and every action, every policy is problematised. All of which illustrates the complexity of the situation but hardly offers a viable way forward. Although most agree that time is of the essence, decisions should be made quickly and action must be taken urgently. But you do need a glimmer of hope to get out of the quagmire and this comes, not from *The Syria Dilemma,* but from *Revolt in Syria*. Starr points out that Syrians have successfully negotiated a variety of fault lines and differences that are now used to identify, divide and separate them. The conflict may look insurmountable, but the determination of the Syrian people should not be underestimated. The very fact that they managed to survive the brutalities of the Assad regime and negotiate the harsh terrains of political, social and sectarian divides, suggests they are more than capable of rebuilding a post-

Assad democratic Syria. Starr's book offers a much needed perspective on the lives of millions of Syrians, left broken and temporarily suspended by the unconventional nature of their surroundings, yet somehow able to carry on. The portrayals of how ordinary people negotiate their way through the current crisis with courage and steadfastness are simply brilliant. They are 'simply seeking a better life' Starr states; and one feels that, despite all the hurdles, they will eventually succeed.

CINEMA OF DEFIANCE

Yasmin Fedda and Daniel Gorman

Syrian-made films are not something new that has just arrived with the uprising. Documentary filmmaking, with its focus on giving an honest portrayal of a situation, has played an important and hotly contested role in Syria for many years. Prior to 2011, Syrian filmmakers were required to seek the permission of the National Film Organisation to make their films and, as such, walked the tightrope of regime whim, never sure if their film would be permitted or banned. The situation changed completely in 2011. Today those making films face imprisonment, torture or death. Bassel Shehadeh, a talented young filmmaker and a personal friend, was killed by a regime shell on 28 May 2012 as he organised filmmaking workshops in Homs. Many others have faced similar fates. And yet, in spite of the huge dangers, there continues to be an outpouring of creative work from Syria, with many choosing to utilise the medium of documentary film.

One of the earliest critical documentaries in Syria was *Khutwa, Khutwa* (Step by Step), by Ousama Mohammed, filmed in 1976–77. It was Mohammed's graduation film for the Geramasov Institute of Cinematography in Moscow, which he attended on a Syrian-state funded scholarship. The film charts the connection between patriarchy and the militarisation of Syrian society, and the effects of both on social relationships. In a song sung by a village elder, what begins like traditional lyrics about the countryside are revealed as total allegiance to Hafez al-Assad. Mohammed develops this theme by following young boys and children in the countryside, charting their transformation from young citizens to soldiers, some of whom are willing to kill for the regime. As a young conscript in the navy proclaims to his friend, while they look over their village from a hill: 'If my brother insulted the party, insulted the leadership... I'd kill him, really I would.' *Khutwa, Khutwa* is a biting critique of the hold of both militarisation and the rule of Assad on everyday village life.

Following *Khutwa, Khutwa*, Mohammed continued to make critical films inside Syria. His 1988 feature film *Nujum al-Nahar* (Stars in Broad Daylight) depicts a rural Alawi family ruled over by a despotic brother who bears a striking resemblance to Hafez al-Assad. Syria scholar Lisa Wedeen hailed *Nujum al-Nahar* as 'perhaps the most politically critical film ever to have been made in Syria'. However, living and working in Syria, Mohammed was obliged to operate under the restrictions of the National Film Organisation, with his films essentially being 'shelved by diktat', neither officially condemned nor available for viewing by the general Syrian public.

The National Film Organisation (NFO) in Syria was originally set up in 1969 by the Ba'athist regime of Salah Jadid to produce state propaganda films, before the coup (or 'Correctionist Movement') that brought Assad to absolute power. Under Assad's reign, the NFO no longer served a direct propaganda function; but by 1974, its head banned the making of documentary films outright, possibly because they were not necessarily based on scripts which could be censored, and were more difficult to control. Omar Amiralay (1944 - 2011) was the only filmmaker who worked with the NFO and yet focussed solely on documentary films. Indeed, his short-lived and always contested affiliation with the organisation could potentially be seen as a reason for the NFO's dislike of the medium.

Amiralay is widely considered to be the founding father of creative documentary in Syria. Born in Damascus, he studied filmmaking in France, where he was inspired by his filming of the quasi-revolutionary events in Paris 1968. He returned to Syria and made his first documentary in 1970: *Film – Muhawalah 'An Sadd al-Furat* (Film – Essay on the Euphrates Dam). It celebrated the construction of the Assad Dam in north eastern Syria as an act of progress and modernisation. But once he had spent more time in Syria, Amiralay's films began to take a much more critical position. *Al-Hayat al Yowmiyyah fi Qaraya Suriyya* (Everyday Life in a Syrian Village), filmed in 1974, was an unflinching portrayal of the government's failure to fulfil the land reforms promised by the Ba'athist revolution. Although the film was funded by the NFO, it was banned upon completion, and remains banned.

After a long and prolific career, much of it pursued outside Syria, Amiralay finally returned to the subject of his first film in 2003 with *Tufan fi Bilad al-Ba'th* (A Flood in Ba'ath Country). A portrait of those affected by the construction of the Assad dam, it is a devastating critique of the Ba'ath regime. When we watched the film with an audience of young Syrians in March 2012, one year into the Syrian uprising, the clearest response was one of laughter, a laughter of defiance. Amiralay wasn't afraid, for instance, to show the ridiculous nature of the regime's totalitarian control of society, poking fun at its rhetoric and symbolism in order to undermine it.

The following films are discussed in this essay:

Khutwa, Khutwa, director, Ousama Mohammed, 1976-77.
Nujum al-Nahar, Director, Ousama Mohammed, 1988.
Film – Muhawalah 'An Sadd al-Furat, director, Omar Amiralay, 1970.
Al-Hayat alYowmiyyah fi Qaraya Suriyya, director, Omar Amiralay, 1974.
Tufan fi Bilad al-Ba'th, director, Omar Amiralay, 2003.
Zabad, director, Reem Ali, 2006.
Hajar al-Aswad, director Nidal al-Dibs, 2006.
Damascus Roof and Tales of Paradise, director Soudade Kadaan, 2010.
MiG, director Thaer al-Sahli, 2013.
Return to Homs, director Talal Derki, 2013. A trailer can be viewed at: http://filmguide.sundance.org/film/13931/return_to_homs
Of Gods and Dogs, director, The Abounaddara Collective, 2013. The Sundance Film Festival prize ceremony can be viewed at: http://www.youtube.com/watch?v=p61qP2jdFOg
Art of Surviving, director Azza Hamwi, 2013. It can be seen here https://www.youtube.com/watch?v=28d1-AgGOW0

The film opens with shots from his previous film and a confession that '33 years ago I was a staunch defender of modernisation in my homeland, Syria', along with clips from his earlier film on the construction of the Assad Dam. It then moves to the sounds of the chanting of children –

'Ready... Pioneers... At Ease... Ba'ath!' These chants recur throughout the film. A key recurring motif is the militarisation of children. At one point the children are asked in catechism, 'Are you ready to sacrifice for it (al-Ba'ath)?' to which they reply 'We are ready!'

'*Tufan fi Bilad al-Ba'th*' provides a glimpse of life within the militarised schooling system which was built under Hafez al-Assad and continued under Bashar al-Assad, a system familiar to Syrians and yet miles away from the modern and enlightened image which Bashaar al-Assad (and his glamorous wife Asma) aimed to project to the international community. Many of the endlessly-repeated chants are led by the children themselves, such as the 'Welcome our Leaders', which occurs mid-way through the film: 'Welcome our leaders, by God you have honoured us, yes you have honoured us, the nicest salute to the leader, everybody listen to us, our pioneers, our sunshine, we salute the leader Bashaar'. A teacher describes how 'as the children chant the principles of the Arab Ba'ath Socialist Party, these principles are implanted in them as a sprout is implanted in fertile soil'. The film was made soon after the death of Hafez al-Assad, and he is frequently referred to in almost mystical terms as 'the great leader, the immortal'. Teachers describe themselves as 'soldiers' in service to 'Comrade Dr. Bashaar Hafez al-Assad'.

Amiralay's masterpiece was never publicly screened inside the country. But it provided an impetus for independent documentary film making in Syria; and its rise has been irresistible.

As small scale digital cameras became more accessible in Syria it became easier for independent filmmakers to make films unofficially. Of particular significance is Reem Ali's Zabad, made with the support of the short-lived Arab Institute of Film, which was headed by Amiralay. Zabad (2006), a biting critique of everyday repression under the Assad regime, tells the story of a couple living in a Syrian coastal town. The wife, Asmahan, looks after her schizophrenic brother; and the film charts their life predominantly through his point of view. Both Asmahan and her husband were once Communist activists and political prisoners. The tension in the film centres on Asmahan being unable to reconcile her past and present, and unable to decide whether to emigrate or stay with her brother. Through an intimate family portrait the film shows the social and political tensions operating in

Syria at the time. Asmahan is constantly under pressure and unable to express herself freely. The political becomes very personal indeed.

A number of other critical documentaries also appeared at this time. *Hajar al-Aswad* by Nidal al-Dibs follows a group of children from the inner-city slum area of Hajar al-Aswad, Damascus, people of a class which rarely appeared in Syrian media. Filmmaker Soudade Kadaan made several documentaries around Damascus for al-Jazeera, beyond NFO control. Her film *Damascus Roof and Tales of Paradise* (2010) looks at the regeneration of old Damascus and the resulting rapid changes in the city's life. Many films of the period turned their cameras on real people's lives and concerns, shining light on life as lived, rather than life as imagined in feature films or TV serials, which Syria was increasingly becoming famous for.

In 2008, when Damascus was the Arab Capital of Culture, Syria's only independent documentary film festival, Dox Box, was founded. During that year a number of cultural projects were permitted across Damascus, with public space made available for artistic ventures. Dox Box made use of this opening to stage their first festival, spread between Damascus, Homs and Tartus, which they managed to develop into an annual project, growing to include Aleppo too. We aimed to 'open a window in Syria for the audience to watch the world and relate to it, and to see films from all walks of life', says Diana al-Jeroudi, co-founder of Dox Box. The festival eventually included over fifty screenings, the very popular Dox Box Campus, a seven-day workshop for documentary work in development from all over the Arab world, and the Tabadol (Exchange) networking event which provided space and time for young Syrian filmmakers to meet with their regional and international counterparts.

Organised as a non-profit, free admission event, Dox Box was a ground-breaking venture. As al-Jeroudi puts it, 'our ultimate goal was to put Syria on the international documentary map. The films we screened included many which touched upon themes rarely discussed in public in Syria, films like *Burma VJ* or *Battle of Chile* or *City of Photographers*, where it's all about revolution and defying censorship, defying state control, defying secret police… All of this was really reflecting a lot of the reality in Syria at that time for the audiences'. Dox Box managed to pull this off by not overstepping the 'threshold', as al-Jeroudi puts it, which of course meant any critical mention of Syria or of the regime's friends, such as Egypt, Tunisia and Iran.

Everything has changed, of course, since 2011. Jeroudi refers to the pre-revolutionary period as 'another century'. As part of the crackdown on dissident voices, Orwa Nyrabia, the other co-founder of Dox Box, was arrested en-route to Damascus airport in August 2012 by the Syrian Military Intelligence and held for three weeks. He stated afterwards that calls from within the international arts community for his release were a successful example of pressure being levelled at the regime. Both he and al-Jeroudi have since been forced to leave Syria; their work, however, continues. As Jeroudi says, 'we should not shut up'. Dox Box has coordinated global solidarity film days for Syria, and Dox Box's parent company, Proaction Film, produced the harrowing long-form documentary *Return to Homs* in late 2013. This film, directed by Talal Derki, follows Abd al-Basset al-Sarout, an up-and-coming football goalkeeper with Karama FC in Homs who has played for Syria's international youth teams. When the revolution erupts, Sarout emerges as a singer at the protests. As the situation becomes more desperate he makes the decision to take up arms to protect his city, which has been under continual regime attack and siege. His uncle and all four of his brothers are killed by the regime, and al-Sarout himself narrowly avoids death. Although only recently completed, the film has drawn international attention, winning the audience award at the 2014 Sundance Festival and opening the International Documentary Film Festival (IDFA) in 2013.

Once the Syrian Uprising began, video activists and filmmakers across the country became active in filming and documenting what was happening to their communities. Filmmakers had to work clandestinely to continue their work as they were being targeted, arrested and sometimes killed by the regime. For obvious reasons, many video activists focused on documentation, for example highlighting the repression of peaceful protests and regime atrocities and war crimes. Footage was generally filmed on people's mobile phones, uploaded to YouTube, and sent to international media networks. These documentation films are generally one-shot affairs, with occasional commentary made by the person filming. The footage is reactive and turned around as quickly as possible in order to show the outside world what is happening inside Syria.

Meanwhile, a smaller group continues the tradition of documentary filmmaking, despite extremely difficult circumstances. Short creative documentaries have continued to emerge from the country since 2011. Whilst these films share something of the immediacy of the news documentation films, they also tell a human story, providing a deeper context for understanding what is happening inside Syria. They are made independently, and are also a product of training and mentorship schemes operating both inside and outside Syria.

Tournesol (Sunflowers) is one of the first short creative documentaries to emerge during the revolutionary period. Made after the siege of al-Rastan in Homs province during the summer of 2011, it is overlaid by interviews with witnesses to the regime assault. All the voices are anonymous. We do not see anyone's face – an effect which creates a haunting, ghost town atmosphere. The only faces we see clearly are those of soldiers who have made the decision to defect from Assad's forces and who have subsequently fought to protect their hometown. Their faces are juxtaposed with scenes of destruction, shots of dying sunflowers and starving kittens. *Tournesol* has been aired on al-Arabiya, the pan-Arab satellite news channel, and uploaded to YouTube.

Films such as *Tournesol* are known as 'situation films'. They are a reaction to realities on the ground, focusing on a specific moment and context. As one of the anonymous directors put it: 'It is your role of taking part in the dramatic experiences of your country … it is a form of work rather than an act of creativity'. However, these films are not purely focused on documentation; they also aim to tell stories, and as a result there are reflective moments in the films, such as the kittens playing in the rubble in *Tournesol*.

Filmmakers continue to live and work inside Syria, usually working anonymously and engaging in grassroots initiatives to share skills and resources and to train new filmmakers. The Abounaddara Collective, for instance, makes 'Emergency Cinema', as they term it, producing one short film a week from inside Syria. Their film *Of Gods and Dogs*, focusing on a young soldier in the Free Syrian Army, won the Grand Jury Prize for short films at the 2014 Sundance Film Festival. *Everyday, Everyday,* made as part of the Hakawati Project, shows an intimate family portrait degenerating into claustrophobia as the conflict escalates. *MiG* by Thaer al-Sahli focuses on the director's neighbourhood Yarmouk, a predominantly Palestinian area of Damascus. Filmed in 2013, this is a love letter both to his wife and to his beloved neighbourhood. A week after al-Sahli marries, the registry office is destroyed by a shell fired from a MiG. His neighbourhood, the area that kept alive his connection to his Palestinian history, is now being destroyed by regime bombardment, and this film is his testimony to the destruction, an act of resistance and of bearing witness. Eyen Film is yet another initiative based inside Syria, an informal workshop which empowers young filmmakers by skill sharing and courses in direction. Eyen Film supported the short film *Art of Surviving* by Azza Hamwi, which follows the work of a man from Douma who turns the shells and artillery fired at his town into art works, musical instruments, and functional objects like toilets and heaters. These initiatives, with a strong do-it-yourself ethic and a focus on allowing the Syrian voice to emerge, reflect the richness of current talent.

Much like the Syrian uprising itself, the outpouring of creative work from Syria since 2011 did not arrive from a void. There have been many brave documentary makers working within the country over the past decades, producing challenging, politically engaged films and laying the ground for what was to come. The key difference now, however, is in the amount of work being produced. The Syrian Revolution began with calls for freedom and dignity. Documentary film continues to be one outlet for these demands, with Syrian voices from across the country representing themselves and speaking on their own behalf, reflecting the diversity of political and artistic life in war-torn Syria.

THE COMPLICITY OF SYRIAN DRAMA

Maysaloon

You would struggle to find an ordinary Syrian who could name their top five Syrian films. This is not because there is a lack of talent in producing such films, but mainly because of economics. Simply put, there is very little return on investment for large film productions in a region that is notorious for software and video piracy and with very little in the way of intellectual property law. Syrian drama serials, on the other hand, have enjoyed a boost in the last fifteen years and have become popular throughout the Middle East. This has been mainly down to two factors: firstly, the proliferation of satellite television stations and receiving equipment throughout the Arab world, and secondly, a boost in both foreign and domestic investment that helped Syrian producers and directors focus their talents towards television dramas. Piracy might still be an issue, but satellite channels, especially those based in the Gulf states, have been able to buy exclusive rights for various dramas during the peak period of television viewing, particularly the month of Ramadan, and have been able to command considerable fees for advertising and sponsorship.

The following serials are discussed in the essay:

Bab al Hara, director, Bassam al-Malla, 2006
The Diaspora, director, Nathir Awwad, 2003
al-Burkan, director, Muhammad Aziziya, 1993
Ayyam Shammiyeh, director, Bassam al-Malla, 1992
Nihayat Rajul Shuja'a, director, Najdat Ismail Anzour, 1993
al-Jawareh, director, Najdat Ismail Anzour, 1994
Ikhwat al Turab, director, Najdat Ismail Anzour, 1996
Ma Malakat Aymanukum, director, Najdat Ismail Anzour, 2010
Ghizlan fi Ghabat al-Thi'ab, director, Rasha Sharbatji, 2006

But despite its popularity, and its economic successes, Syrian drama is still fundamentally flawed. This is because it operates both under a ceiling of government approval and direction, and also under its own limits of self-censorship. Thus we cannot talk about Syrian drama without understanding Syrian politics, because the former has been shaped by the latter almost since its inception and has played a vital role in shaping the perceptions of the Syrian public and their relationship both with their government and the outside world.

The tone was set by *Bab al Hara* (The Neighbourhood Gate). Indeed, it can be argued that it was this 2006 series which brought Syrian drama serials and comedy back into the international Arabic limelight. In homes across the region, families would settle down to watch the historical drama which was set in a traditional Damascus neighbourhood during the French occupation. It became, in effect, a Ramadan institution, and heralded a flood of similar historical dramas as well as comedies and more topical series relating to social issues.

It is worth remembering that prior to 2011 Syria was enjoying an almost unprecedented appreciation and popularity throughout the Arab world. Projecting an image of a modernising Arab president pursuing a self-professed 'resistance' foreign policy, particularly against Israel and the West, Assad's regime had allied itself with Iran to solidify its position whilst maintaining links with Arab countries that it did not agree with. Following the Iranian and Syrian-backed Hizbullah's defeat of Israel in Lebanon in 2006, the Syrian regime felt at its most confident. The rhetoric coming out of Damascus in those years was one of triumph. It was in this political milieu that pre-revolutionary Syrian drama found its popularity. The themes of dramas defined Syrian popular culture in those years.

Triumphalism notwithstanding, Syrian directors, artists and writers had to work within the now infamous 'red lines' that were known but never spoken of. Everyone was aware that saying or writing the 'wrong' thing, regardless of intention, could easily result in incarceration or even being killed. This tension might have eased after the death of Assad's father in 2000, but after almost forty years of Ba'athist rule most people had learned never to assume anything or to take any chances. And even during this 'triumphalist' phase writers wisely recalled the fate of people who had inadvertently strayed from the acceptable narrative, and who paid for their sin with long prison sentences, the case of the schoolgirl Tal al-Malouhi, jailed for blogging poems about Palestine, being particularly pertinent. Of course such incarcerations were politely ignored in society, and Syrian producers and film makers were no different. If the repression caused them any discomfort, they didn't mention it in public.

Under these circumstances, Syrian drama played a critical role for the Syrian regime by providing a space for '*tanfis*' or letting society breathe through slight acknowledgement of its predicament. Syrian viewers were given a sense of all being in it together, being part of a mass system which, though undoubtedly problematic, constituted a coherent whole of some sort and therefore a locus for solidarity and loyalty. It is hardly surprising that the Syrian regime would want to promote such a vision. What is more startling is seeing it internalised by the writers and directors of these serials and then presented to the Syrian audience in a digestible form. We can only speculate that direct links existed between the directors of these shows and shadowy departments in the Syrian regime which drew up these narratives and then doled them out. We may never know the true extent of the collusion between the Syrian regime and the television industry, but it would not be an exaggeration to say that it is undoubtedly extensive and considerable.

There are very clear themes in Syrian dramas, particularly the ones that deal with political or historical issues. As these shows became more sophisticated, their method of delivering narratives not only became more subtle, but they felt able to go further in the kind of message that they sought to portray. One disturbing example that illustrates the level of political infiltration is *The Diaspora*, which depicted some of the worst anti-Semitic stereotypes, including the vulgar 'blood libel' myth. Broadcast by Hizbullah's propaganda channel al-Manar, the series is said to be inspired by the book *The Matzah of Zion* written by Syria's then defence minister, Mustafa Tlass. Tlass claims that Jews used the blood of children in Damascus to make a particular type of bread in a secret rite. Segments of this anti-Semitic serial are still available on YouTube. They make for unsettling viewing.

Slightly less twisted, but just as disturbing, is the approach used by many in the Syrian film and television industry to shape a narrative of 'acceptable' political discourse. In the 1980s a popular series called *al-Burkan* (The

Volcano) narrated the story of a weak Arabian tribe, one of many that were divided and oppressed by the Romans, who finally unite under a strong leader and became powerful enough to defy the empire. The theme is a popular one in Syrian drama, and the idea of a foreign enemy scheming and capitalising on the weaknesses and divisions of the Arabs, or oppressing them through their laws, is arguably one that is deeply embedded in popular culture. In the series *Bab al-Hara*, for example, a distinction was repeatedly made between the laws of the French Mandate's administration and the 'laws' of the neighbourhood, the local laws. Crimes and transgressions are dealt with 'locally' by the head of the neighbourhood and his strong man, the *ageed*. The preference is always given to 'local justice', and the neighbourhood is considered as a family – patriarchal of course – in which problems are kept away from the prying eyes of foreigners. All these subtle cues are buried in the dodging and weaving of well-thought plots that keep viewers hooked. But during the eighties Syrian drama serials did not have either the sophistication or the enormous pan-Arab audience that they would enjoy twenty years later, and most productions from that time are relatively crude affairs.

The really exciting innovations came later, firstly with serials such as *Ayyam Shammiyeh* (Damascus Days), a precursor to *Bab al Hara*, which became an instant hit for its excellent script, character development and storyline. It was during this time that Syrian dramas began to gain popularity with the domestic audience that had grown used to watching Egyptian serials. And in this period drama serials became Syria's most easily-recognised export to the Arab world, even overtaking the Egyptian brand. Syrian histories, historical fantasies, family dramas and comedies touched a pan-Arab chord. Syrian characters and actors became household names from Casablanca to Muscat, from Khartoum to Mosul.

This change was probably crystallised with the arrival of the renowned Syrian director Najdat Ismail Anzour. A Circassian, Anzour came up with *Nihayat Rajul Shuja'a* (The End of a Brave Man), a series set in the French mandate. His coup was in introducing action and special effects on a level that was almost comically surprising to many Syrians – and they loved it. The series itself was a confusing affair; nobody could quite say precisely why or how Anzour's hero was brave, but it was a big production. The slick picture quality, gorgeous scenery, and the innovative special effects, brought something very new to the Syrian audience. Here was a Syrian historical drama which showed spectacular battle scenes (against the occupying French) and fight scenes at a level of professionalism which surprised jaded viewers. It was something different and new. The rousing song for the opening theme, something that Syrian dramas today are particularly good at, became instantly popular.

Anzour followed with another ambitious project called *al-Jawareh* (The Birds of Prey). This series did not have the same degree of success, but once again it brought big production values to its subject – this time a fictional historical setting based on inter-tribal rivalry. The brightest spotlight was shone on Anzour after he directed the series *Ikhwat al-Turab* (Brothers of the Soil). Set in Syria during the First World War (still referred to by Syrians as the days of the *Safarbarlik*), this depiction of the Armenian genocide provoked an outcry from neighbouring Turkey, and was very likely the first time that the subject had been dealt with and presented to an Arab audience. This was no small matter, especially in an authoritarian state like Syria.

During the 1990s, Bashaar al-Assad's father Hafez had extremely tense relations with Turkey over his support for the radical Kurdish PKK movement and its leader Abdullah Ocalan. Only a few years later Turkey and Syria almost went to war over the matter, but Hafez reluctantly agreed to exile Ocalan and curtail his support for the PKK's armed campaign in Turkish Kurdistan. It is easy to speculate, therefore, that this supposed example of risk-taking openness was actually an act of collaboration with regime priorities – not so much a case of art examining power as of power exploiting art. Anzour would later court controversy during the Syrian revolution over his lurid depiction of the Saud family – again, the timing was extremely convenient. Bashaar was now locked in a struggle with Saudi Arabia, whom he blamed for the Syrian uprising and for arming and supplying Islamist oppositional fighters.

In another drama, *Ma Malakat Aymanukum* (What Your Right Arm has Conquered), released only shortly before the Syrian revolution erupted, he approached the controversial topics of honour killings and Islamic extremism. (One of the writers who worked on that series is academic and presenter of the Egyptian talk show *Lady of Ladies*, Hala Diyab. These days Diyab lives in the United Kingdom, where on the BBC's 'Newsnight' she pleaded with the public and government not to allow Syrian refugees into the country because, she claimed, they are incapable of assimilating.) The drama was received well but by this time more daring topics, including government corruption, were not uncommon on Syrian television.

In *Ghizlan fi Ghabat al Thi'ab* (Gazelles in a Forest of Wolves), for example, Rasha Sherbatji, a female director, delivered a series that showed Syrians what had previously been an unspoken secret – the abuses and corruption of members of government. It contained cryptic references to 'the Party' and even 'the leadership' of the party, although the person and name of the Syrian president remained inviolable. The show was well received but it is important, once again, to note the timing and context within which it was permitted. By 2008 Bashaar al-Assad had been in power for eight years and, despite expanding cronyism in the newly neo-liberal economy, was still trying to maintain an image of himself as a reformer combatting corruption. So at a time when the Syrian regime was anxious to portray itself as modernising, liberalising, and stamping down on corruption, a series of shows emerged which portrayed a well-intentioned 'leadership' being let down by corrupt and incompetent officials. These functionaries are perceived as the real source of misery for the average Syrian. The language used, far from being condescending, is actually seductive in its simplicity, and the genius of such political narratives is that they no longer take the blunt rhetorical approach of earlier eras, but are embedded in love stories, emotional struggles and personal dilemmas.

There's nothing new in totalitarian regimes seeking to dominate all avenues of public life in the countries under their control. Nowhere was this more apparent than in the cultural policies of Eastern Europe and the Soviet Union, and it is still very much alive in Putin's Russia today. (Hafez al-Assad's repressive apparatus was designed with the help of Soviet-era Russian and East German advisors, and Russia remains a collaborator of Bashaar's today, in the propaganda field as much as in funding and arms.) What is remarkable in Syria, however, is the extent to which the illusion of a functioning public 'dialogue' and an artistic, creative and political scene was created, so that entire opposition camps, media outlets and the film industry were replicated in a miniature cosmos of acceptable party parameters and discourse.

The Assad regime under father and son has had over forty years to completely subvert Syrian public life – to dominate everything from students and workers' unions to the press, the universities and the schools. The same must hold true for the Syrian television industry. The parallels between the regime's different political stances, especially over the past thirteen years, and the themes tackled by Syrian television shows are striking.

What of the future? The national trauma that Syria is undergoing as it excises Assad's regime will undoubtedly have a major effect on its drama and production. Much has certainly been lost over the past three years – lives, funds, often the public space itself. But to imagine that Syrian film and drama could ever have fulfilled its creative potential or truly thrived as a questioning mirror to society is to put faith in a fallacy. There can be no qualitative comparison between what a truly free Syrian film industry could one day achieve and the regime's tainted construction that we witnessed before 2011.

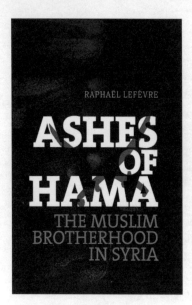

RAPHAËL LEFÈVRE

ASHES OF HAMA
The Muslim Brotherhood in Syria

RAPHAËL LEFÈVRE

When the convulsions of the Arab Spring first became manifest in Syria in March 2011, the Ba'athist regime was quick to blame the protests on the 'Syrian Muslim Brotherhood' and its 'al-Qaeda affiliates.' But who are these Islamists so determined to rule a post-Assad Syria?

ISBN: 9781849042857
£30.00 / Hardback / 288pp

Little has been published on militant Islam in Syria since Hafez Assad's regime destroyed the Islamist movement in its stronghold of Hama in February 1982. This book bridges that gap by providing readers with the first comprehensive account of the Syrian Muslim Brotherhood's history to date.

In this groundbreaking account of Syria's most prominent, yet highly secretive, Islamist organisation, the author draws on previously untapped sources: the memoirs of former Syrian jihadists; British and American archives; and also a series of wide-ranging interviews with the Syrian Muslim Brotherhood's historical leaders as well as those who battled against them—many speaking on the record for the first time. Ashes of Hama uncovers the major aspects of the Islamist struggle: from the Brotherhood's radicalisation and its 'jihad' against the Ba'athist regime and subsequent exile, to a spectacular comeback at the forefront of the Syrian revolution in 2011—a remarkable turnaround for an Islamist movement which all analysts had pronounced dead amid the ruins of Hama in 1982.

'No book could be more timely than Lefèvre's on the Muslim Brotherhood. Anyone wishing to understand Syria must understand the long and bitter history of the Muslim Brotherhood's struggle with the Assad regime.' — Joshua M. Landis, Director, Center for Middle East Studies, University of Oklahoma, and author of Syria Comment

WWW.HURSTPUBLISHERS.COM/BOOK/ASHES-OF-HAMA

HURST
PUBLISHERS

41 GREAT RUSSELL ST, LONDON WC1B 3PL
WWW.HURSTPUBLISHERS.COM
WWW.FBOOK.COM/HURSTPUBLISHERS
020 7255 2201

ET CETERA

ON RELIGIOUS ENVIRONMENTALISM

Ehsan Masood

We are at the very beginning of what could be the most serious environmental crisis since the last great Mass Extinction. For the uninitiated, a Mass Extinction is when a significant number of plant and animal species become extinct in a short space of geological time. The last, and the fifth, was 65 million years ago; a possible reason, it is argued, is that a meteorite hit Earth. Many scientists now think that we may be heading for a sixth Mass Extinction – unlike those in the past, this will be entirely man-made. It is unlikely to happen tomorrow, or next month, or next year. It is early stages – but the signs are unmistakable.

If you look at one indicator of the health of Planet Earth you will see what I mean: that indicator is extinction itself. In the two centuries between 1600 and 1800, some 38 species of birds and mammals have become extinct. Between 1810 and 1995 that climbed to 112 species. A prominent group of conservation biologists thinks that one fifth of all living populations could become extinct within the next 30 years.

Extinction is natural – not all species can survive or move to new environments if they are threatened. At the same time, not all extinction is bad and some extinction is completely desirable for human survival and wellbeing. No one wants polio or smallpox hanging around; and we all want to see eradication – or at least better control – of the mosquito that causes malaria. But the consensus among scientists is that our current extinction rates are way more than we might expect them to be: a hundred times the background, maybe more. This is a similar consensus to that on climate change: that, unless something is done quickly, global temperatures will continue to rise leading to more extreme weather events, such as floods and droughts.

Why is this happening now? In a nutshell, the reasons for our present environmental crisis have much to do with industrialisation. Our modern lifestyles mean that humans have changed how we use the land. Species become threatened when we clear land for farming on an industrial scale and when we use chemicals on the land; they become threatened when we build housing developments for expanding populations and for the increasingly smaller households that are a feature of modern life.

A decade or so ago, world leaders promised to take steps to slow down the rate of species decline and to do so by 2010. In addition, ongoing talks on climate change promised similar action. The international community has also sought the help of faith groups. All over the world large networks of faith-based organisations are being mobilised to spread the message that religions, all religions, are inherently environmentalist. All religions emphasise stewardship of nature and see environmental conservation as an act of piety.

There is a delicious irony in this. It may be controversial, but we need to appreciate that religion, particularly Christianity and Islam, have played an important part in our present environmental crisis.

Much of the technology we take for granted today emerged during the age of Europe's great empires: electricity, the internal combustion engine, the birth of telecommunications. They coincided with a time when Europe had the confidence, the money and the military power to be able to look far beyond its borders. European men travelled and conquered. They spread science and they also spread religion.

One of my favourite books is called the *Science of Empire*. It is by an American sociologist called Zaheer Baber who tells the story of how Britain brought modern science to India. It has been nearly twenty years since I first reviewed it in *Nature*, yet this is one of those books that I still find myself dipping in and out of. Baber spent years burrowing through archives of what used to be the India Office library in London. Peppered through his accounts of the creation of botanical gardens, professional scientific societies, and official scientific advisory boards are some gems which provide flashes of insight into the motivations of those involved in the colonial project. Here is an example from Sir Charles Trevelyan: 'the peculiar wonder of the [sic] Hindu system is not that it contains so much or so little of true knowledge, but that it has been so skilfully contrived to arrest the progress of the human mind. Our duty is not to teach, but to unteach'. Or this from Charles Grant: 'by planting our knowledge, our opinions and our religion in our Asiatic territories, we shall put a great work beyond social contingencies'. The religion that Grant is speaking of is Christianity. But this is Christianity in a particular social and historical context. It is the Christianity of empire and of the industrial revolution.

A little over four decades ago, Lynn White Jr, an American Christian priest and historian of the Middle Ages, wrote a seminal essay for *Science*. It was called: 'The Historical Roots of Our Ecological Crisis'. White argued controversially that Christianity was effectively responsible for the environmental crisis; and essentially presented three arguments. First, he believed that the idea of progress, of perpetual and constant improvement, is partly rooted in the Christianity of the industrial revolution. Second, that because nature and God cannot be linked in Christianity, as they are in many folk religions, this provides a cover for Christians to be able to use and abuse the natural world without committing an act of desecration, or sin. And third, White argued that one particular text of the Bible had perhaps done the most harm, the famous line from Genesis: 'Then God blessed them, and said to them, "Be fruitful and multiply; fill the earth and subdue it; have dominion over the fish of the sea, over the birds of the air, and over every living thing that moves on the earth"' (Genesis 1:28).

So one could say that industrial revolution and religion together must share the blame for the predicament that we find ourselves in today. But that is only the half of the story.

Something very interesting has been happening since White's *Science* paper caused the firestorm that it did. This is the emergence – some would say re-emergence – of a strong tradition of Christian environmental ethics. It can be summarised by the following words from an Australian clergyman: 'the outcome of the case of The Earth v Christianity was that Christianity, having been found guilty of complicity in ecocide, was ordered to re-enter the struggle for global survival – only this time on the side of the Earth'.

And so over the past few decades there has emerged what some would call Green Christianity; or Christian environmentalism. And its proponents point to alternate passages from the scripture, which support the idea that humans are God's stewards; that humans do not own nature, but are its guardians, trustees, even tenants. For anyone who wheels out Genesis 1:28, the answer comes back as Leviticus 25:23 in which God says: 'The land must not be sold permanently because the land is mine and you are but aliens and my tenants'.

Green Christians are a growing movement, and they are working closely within the scientific mainstream. One of the first groups to support the scientific consensus on global warming was the World Council of Churches. They have been active in mobilising congregations and they have an official presence at UN climate talks. Three years ago the Evangelical Climate Initiative was born in the US, signed by eighty-six individuals and organisations, and its supporters now include several prominent American televangelists including Pat Robertson.

So a shift is taking place within Christianity in response to evidence about human responsibility in altering the environment. But what of Islam? Well, Islam, too, is changing, though in many ways it has less far to travel.

It is, at least in theory, relatively easy to be a Muslim environmentalist. Islam has an established and ingrained stewardship ethic. Children are taught from an early age to think of themselves as trustees of God's Earth. Many Muslims will be able to confirm that we need to tread lightly, to use resources carefully, and to consider public interest, equity and the needs of future generations when allocating resources. Islam's first environmentalists included the Prophet himself, his younger cousin Ali, and there are many, many recorded examples from the lives of the first generation of Muslims that illustrate practice of what they preached. The Prophet declared, 'the world is green and beautiful and God has appointed you His stewards over it'.

Perhaps one reason why Islamic environmentalism has had less far to travel is the absence of a strong tradition of anthropocentrism – though it is not entirely free from this phenomenon. For example, astronomers from the Islamic era believed that the Earth was at the centre of creation, but they came close to embracing the idea of a Sun-centred Universe. Moreover, when that particular revolution happened, to my knowledge, there was no major controversy about displacing Man and Earth from the centre of creation.

In a similar way the eleventh-century Spanish Sufi mystic ibn Arabi developed an idea that he called the Unity of Existence or Unity of Being. In this he suggested that God and creation are essentially one and the same.

If Islamic environmentalism has a second keystone tradition, I would say that this would be Sufism. And it is interesting to see that some of today's leading Muslim environmental thinkers of the Western world – people such as Seyyed Hossein Nasr of Georgetown University or Fazlun Khalid, the founder of the Islamic Foundation for Ecology and Environmental Sciences – come from within the Sufi tradition.

When I was researching my book *Science and Islam: A History*, I was keen to talk to people about the origins of Sufism – in part because Sufism is also at the centre of one of the great controversies of Islamic history, the debate between the theologian al Ghazali and the philosopher ibn Rushd (Averroes) about the limits of rational thinking. This is a debate that is seen by many scientists to have sowed an anti-science sentiment in the Islamic world.

Somewhat naively, I expected to read about pious patrons, caliphs and emirs, who were turned on by the spirit of inquiry and who wanted to invest in knowledge for the sake of it. That is true to some extent. But also true is that their desire for knowledge came via a lust for power. This was knowledge in the service of empire-building. Some of Islam's scientific patrons were convinced that they were the heirs to an exciting, new, rational system of belief and practice. They regarded Christianity and Judaism as the old order. Islam was cutting-edge and they believed that they had a duty to spread scientific thinking via Islam among their populations and beyond. They were often highly intolerant of anyone who disagreed with them and they lived ostentatious lifestyles.

What does all of this tell us? Well at the very least it tells us that if Islam is supposed to make it easy to be an environmentalist our history does not make it obvious. Many Muslim rulers were far from ideal ecologists.

So much for the past, what of today?

Some years ago, Yale University in the US listed every country in what it calls an Environmental Performance Index. Countries were scored according to a number of indicators such as air quality, water resources, biodiversity and habitat protection, and the development of clean and sustainable energy sources. Each of these scores was then compressed into a single number – an index. The top score is 100, the lowest is zero.

In 2009, the best performing Islamic country was Malaysia, ninth overall in the world. Other than Malaysia there are no more Muslim countries in the global top ten. Or the top twenty. There are only six in the top fifty. Around half are ranked below that. Iran is fifty-third; Saudi Arabia is fifty-ninth; Indonesia is seventy-ninth; Egypt is eighty-fifth and Pakistan, the world's newest Islamic state, is fifth from the bottom at 127.

So while theology may technically make it easy to be a Muslim environmentalist, the practice of Muslim states is otherwise. The reasons why the environmental record is so dire often has little to do with religion. The richer Islamic countries are threatened by environmentalism because they have oil – in fact often that is all they have.

As a science reporter in the mid-1990s, I attended numerous conferences of climate scientists and UN climate negotiators. This was the period running up to the Kyoto Protocol in which the international community eventually agreed to make cuts in greenhouse gas emissions. Saudi Arabia was not interested in doing anything about climate change. Neither was Iran. In a curious twist of fate both found themselves on the same side as the US and the three joined forces to block a global climate deal. When interviewing the negotiator from Saudi Arabia or Iran, I would always ask: So you come from an Islamic state? Tell me what Islam has to say about protecting nature. One delegate from Saudi Arabia told me: 'that is religion; this is politics'.

What is even more interesting, however, is how Islamic environmentalism is mirroring what happened in Christianity. Remember how Christian theology had to adapt; how the view that man has dominion over nature had to give way to man the steward – and mostly because of mounting scientific evidence that humans are interfering in the climate. Well Islamic theology too is being forced to change – though not necessarily in a good way.

Take the example of water. In Islamic traditions, water is seen as the basis of all life and is regarded as a gift from God. There is strong evidence that the Prophet determined that people will not be charged for drawing water out of wells. This he meant as a way of ensuring that poorer people were not exploited by wealthier well-owners. In other words Islamic theology does not support water-pricing.

Yet today, because of the pressures of population and consumption, water is becoming ever scarcer and most developed countries now charge consumers for water. The drier countries of the Middle East are even more susceptible to water shortages. This is why they have decided to follow suit and put a dollar value on a litre of water. The question is: how to do this in states governed by sharia – when sharia says water is a free good.

What is happening is that Islamic theology is being adapted to support water pricing in developing countries. Both Iran and Saudi Arabia have introduced water pricing. But the justification for this is not that water is in short supply and hence something needs to be done – it is that God will essentially be happy with the principle of putting a price on a litre of water as a way of meeting demand when water is scarce. And that because we are living in different times to that of the first Muslims, we should embrace this change and not complain about God's laws being violated.

Muslim scholars have revised their opinions on the basis of what they see as new evidence from the latest research. But the 'evidence' on which theologians are being asked to change an enlightened centuries-old principle is not at all clear; nor does it represent an expert consensus. There is in fact no consensus among scientists and economists on whether water pricing – or indeed water privatisation – is going to lead us to greener pastures. Many development NGOs regard an Islamic endorsement for water pricing as the misuse of religion.

So, following Christianity, Muslim theologians, too, are adapting how they interpret faith in the light of new evidence. This is partly because those who have faith will not take action unless what is being asked of them can be backed up with evidence from sacred texts. Hence the lengthening queues of scientists, conservationists and politicians at the door of theologians – all trying to get them to see their point of view. But not all viewpoints, including those of the theologians, are beneficial for the environment.

TEN THINGS TO REMEMBER
ABOUT SYRIA

In the pre-revolution days, Syrians were ever ready to list ten of their favourite picnic spots, ten of their much-loved restaurants, or even ten of the sects participating in the imaginary happy mosaic. Today, lists of traumatisation leap to the mind: the ten largest refugee camps, or ten major massacres, or perhaps ten of the numerous new militias.

This list tends towards the positive (only number 10 is a bad thing, but it's something that cannot be ignored). It focuses on those aspects of Syrian reality that can't be destroyed by war, things of enduring value that will survive (with the exception, we hope, of number 10).

1. Maté

Along with Turkish Coffee, Argentinian Yerba Maté is Syria's quintessential drink. Drink it strong and sugary in a gourd or a glass, through a silver straw from the Qalamoun region; keep the water hot for continual fill-ups; and you'll be telling Homsi and *muhashish* jokes all night. Maté connotes conviviality, and sometimes more specifically the Druze, Christian and Alawi mountain communities. When the martyred Free Army commander Abu Furat appealed to the Alawi community, he did so in terms every Syrian would understand: 'I know the Alawis well. I've visited them in their houses. We've drunk maté together. We lived together before and we'll live together again, despite you, Bashaar.'

How did a South American drink become a Syrian (and Lebanese) staple? The answer is to be found in the late-nineteenth and early-twentieth-century mass migration of Syrian-Lebanese to South and North America, the Caribbean, and West Africa. A couple of hundred drowned with the Titanic. The 'Street of the Turks' in Gabriel Garcia Marquez's fictional town Macondo, described in *One Hundred Years of Solitude*, is so-called because the people were Ottomans when they arrived in Colombia, but they were Syrian Ottomans, Arabs. Today 20 million people describe themselves as Syrian-Brazilians. Guyana's richest family is the Maqdeesis. Carlos Menem, former Argentinian president, is of Syrian origin too.

2. Migrants

Abdul-Qadir al-Jaza'iri (1808–1883), the religious and military leader, led a long and heroic resistance against the French occupation of Algeria. Eventually captured and brought to Paris, he was given the choice of exile elsewhere in the Arab world. Abdul-Qadir chose Damascus, where he wrote Sufi poetry in the shrine of the mystic Ibn 'Arabi, who was an earlier migrant, from Andalucía. In 1860, when the Christian quarter of the Old City was burnt in sectarian rioting, Abdul-Qadir protected hundreds of Christians in his house and garden.

The tomb of Ibn 'Arabi stands between two inner-city neighbourhoods climbing the slope of Mount Qassiyoun: 'Muhajireen', or Migrants, is so-named because it once housed Muslim refugees from the Balkans; and 'Akrad' means Kurds – still a Kurdish area, it was first built for the Kurds who came with Salahudeen al-Ayyubi (Saladin's) armies during the twelfth century.

Who else? Armenians, descendants of those who survived the forced march from Anatolia. Half a million registered Palestinian refugees and many more Palestinian-Syrians (Yarmouk camp in Damascus, Syria's largest Palestinian population, is nearly empty now – its population refugees for a second time, mostly in Lebanon). Over a million and a half Iraqi refugees until Damascus and Aleppo became even less secure than Baghdad and Basra. And in 2006, a million refugees from the Lebanese South (fleeing Israeli bombs), were welcomed in mosques, schools and private homes. Syrians angrily compare the way they welcomed refugees with the way they are now (not) welcomed, in their hour of need.

3. Sufis

Talking of Ibn 'Arabi (1165–1240), that most famous and strangest of mystics is by no means the only holy buried in Syria. The tombs of the friends of God crowd old markets, dot hilltops, sit next to streams. From Ghazali (1058–1111) to Suhrawardi (1155–1191), some of the most prominent figures of both sober and drunk traditions of Sufism passed through the country, considering it a way station to Mecca and a holy land in its own right.

'Drunken' Sufis were still a common feature of Syrian streets until recent decades. Private *zikr* sessions and Sufi-influenced *nasheed* and *moulid* singing continue to play an important role in urban life.

But Ibn Taymiyya (1263–1328), the noted theologian, was in Syria too. In Aleppo he decided the blame for the Mongol sack of Baghdad lay with Shi'ism and other such heresies. His anti-Shia, anti-Sufi theology led eventually to Wahhabism. Today the quietism of the traditionalist *ulema* – most notably Mufti Ahmad Badreddin Hassoun and the assassinated Shaikh Ramadan Bouti, both of whom preached loyalty to the regime even as the regime murdered, burnt and raped – has been a major factor in the spread of activist Salafism amongst Syrians. Other clerics of Sufi background, however, such as Muhammad al-Yaqoubi, who speaks out against the regime and against sectarian extremism, have taken much more positive positions.

4. Poetry

And talking of Sufis… Syrian poet Adonis in his wonderful book *Sufism and Surrealism* holds that ecstatic Sufi pronouncements as well as the self-consciously 'written' court poetry of the classical past represented a subjective counter-culture to Arab-Islamic literalism and orthodoxy. Over the centuries, Syria has certainly suffered no shortage of flamboyantly subjective poets, Nizar Qabbani and Muhammad al-Maghout the most important of the late twentieth century.

Tenth-century poet al-Mutanabbi (his name means 'the pretend prophet' because he made messianic claims while leading a Qarmatian revolt) came from Kufa in Iraq but spent his most productive period in Aleppo – before being killed by a man insulted by his verses. The eleventh-century blind poet Abu Ala'a al-Ma'arri (973–1058) was a vegan and an atheist. He witnessed religious war, including Crusader cannibalism in his home town Ma'arat al-Nowman. None of it endeared him to religion:

> Humanity follows two global sects:
> One, man intelligent, without religion,
> The second, man religious, without intellect.

Despite his unorthodox views, al-Ma'arri was highly respected at the time. But Salafist extremists beheaded al-Ma'arri's statue – to great local outrage – in 2013. The statue of the great ninth-century poet Abu Tammam (788–845) was also executed in his southern hometown, Jassim. And the revolutionary poet Ibrahim Qashoush's vocal chords – flesh, not metal – were ripped out by the regime.

Abu Ala'a al-Ma'ari provided a warning for today's desperate situation:

> But some hope a divine leader with prophetic voice
> Will rise amid the gazing silent ranks.
> An idle thought! There's none to lead but reason,
> To point the morning and the evening ways.

5. Fatteh

Damascus and particularly Aleppo are famous for their haute-cuisine, and used to boast some truly world-class restaurants, but the 'working man's food' of Syria is just as good in cheap cafés. The queen of cheap dishes is *fatteh* – strips of bread and chickpeas soaked in oil and yoghurt, with hummus paste and pomegranate, sometimes with mince or even sheep's feet. It's supposed to set you up for solid work, but has the exact opposite effect on most.

Syrian olive oil is good enough to drink neat, and some country people do. The eggs – we swear – are richer and tastier than eggs anywhere else, the chickens less bland, the fruit more juicy. Ask any Syrian, they'll tell you the same.

6. Makdous

This is one of the things that make exile so hard for Syrians – the *makdous* you find outside the country is never like the *makdous* inside. Like *araq*, makdous is best made at home. Most Syrian families know someone who knows someone who makes *makdous* – stuffing aubergines with nuts and peppers and pickling them in olive oil.

Shingleesh, Syria's uranium (actually balls of strong rotten cheese impregnated with spices, best eaten with tomatoes, onions, and oil), is the same – best home-made, and never as good outside the country.

7. 'amiyeh

From the Damascene drawl (*lek shooooooo? Waaaaaynaaak?*) to Bedouin 'hasaniya', the various Syrian colloquialisms make up Syrian *'amiyeh*, the common speech. Textured with pre-Arabic Semitic, especially Aramaic, words and rhythms, and laced with endearments (men as well as women address each other as 'my dear', 'my moon', 'my life', 'o love of my heart'), polite formulae, gritty obscenities, and pepperings of poetry and scripture, it's no surprise the other Arabs prize Syrian Arabic in particular – a boon to the country's actors, poets and news presenters.

Syria is also a great place to study Arabic – not only are the people hospitable, they will even make an effort to speak *fus-ha* (classical Arabic) to students. For that matter, it's a great place to learn some Kurdish, Armenian, Turkmen, Syriac, or Aramaic (which still survives in the Ma'aloula region) – there's just a little problem with bombs at the moment...

8. Upside-down Writing in the Walls

You can see Greek script upside down in the walls of the Umawi Mosque in Damascus. Before it was a mosque it was a cathedral (it still houses the head of John the Baptist); before it was a cathedral it was a Roman-style temple to Jupiter; before that, a temple to Haddad, the Aramean thunder god. Those ancient stones are beneath and around you as you sit in the prayer hall.

Syria contains remnants of Sumerian, Babylonian, Assyrian, Hittite, Greek, Roman, Persian, Macedonian, Umawi, Ayyubid, Zengid, Ottoman and French civilisations, among others. The world's best preserved medieval European castle – Qala'at al-Hosn or Krak des Chevalliers – is not in Europe but near Homs, on the edge of an old Crusading principality. The world's first alphabet (Phoenician) was excavated north of Lattakia. The country is pocked with *tells*, hills made of millennia of human habitation. The pebbles beneath your feet are not pebbles but the shards of ten million pots manufactured and discarded generation after generation after generation.

9. The Nowfara

The Nowfara is the best-known of the traditional cafés in Damascus. Here you can hear the *hakawati* (storyteller) roar and clatter his sword while you sip at your *zuhurat* (a herbal drink), puff the *argileh* (water pipe), and watch the world pass. In every city and town there's a café on every street, a place where you (if you're a man, usually) can refresh yourself while reading the newspaper, playing games, or gossiping. There are bars and restaurants which serve *araq*, Syria's favourite spirit, and there are musical nights, either in a restaurant or laid on at home alongside someone playing an *oud*. Along with weddings, family visits and picnics, the Eids and Christmas, Syria's social life is rich.

10. Men in White Socks

The antithesis of social life, the various branches of the *mukhabarat* or secret police, and their network of informers, were omnipresent in Assad's Syria. Some wear white socks and shiny suits; some leather jackets hoisted to show a gun. Some are enormous, and many Syrians have formative memories of their fists. Some drive the Mercedes 'Ghost' – and that's one origin of the *shabeeha* word used to describe pro-Assad death squads today, from *shabah*, 'ghost'. Many informers are taxi drivers, or school teachers, or the shopkeepers who stay open long hours, and at least one colleague in your office environment. You never quite know who might be writing a report...

Syria's revolution was not provoked by an American-Zionist-Saudi cabal, as the conspiracy theorists claim, but by these men in white socks, and their clumsy, casual brutality.

CITATIONS

Introduction: The Roots of the Syrian Crisis by Peter Clark

I have made many visits to Syria between December 1962 and April 2011, and was living in Damascus from 1992 to 1997. In addition to conversations and observations I have benefited from the growing literature on the recent history and politics of Syria, in particular: Fouad Ajami, *The Syrian Rebellion* (Hoover Institution Press, Stanford, Cal., 2012); Warwick Ball, *Rome in the East* (Routledge, London and New York, 2007; first published, 2000); Hanna Batatu, *Syria's Peasantry, the Descendants of its Lesser Rural Notables, and their Politics*, (Princeton University Press, 1999); Miriam Cooke, *Dissident Syria* (Duke University Press, Durham NC and London, 2007); Peter Clark, *Marmaduke Pickthall British Muslim* (Quartet Books London, 1986); Charles M Doughty, *Travels in Arabia Deserta* (Jonathan Cape, London, 1933; first published 1888); Leila Fawaz, *An Occasion for War: Civil Conflict in Lebanon and Damascus in 1860* (University of California Press, Berkeley, 1994); Philip S Khoury, *Syria and the French Mandate* (Princeton University Press, 1989); Philip S Khoury, *Urban Notables and Arab Nationalism* (Cambridge University Press, 1983); Eberhard Kienle (editor), *Contemporary Syria* (British Academic Press, London, 1994); Fred H Lawson, *Demystifying Syria* (Saqi, London, 2009); David W Lesch, Syria, *The Fall of the House of Assad* (Yale University Press, New Haven and London, 2012); Moshe Ma'oz and others (editors), *Modern Syria* (Sussex Academic Press, London and Portland, 1999); David Roberts, *The Ba'th and the Creation of Modern Syria* (Croom Helm, London, 1987); Christa Salamandra, *A New Old Damascus* (Indiana University Press, Bloomington, 2004); Linda Schatkowski Schilcher, *Families in Politics, Damascene Factions and Estates of the 18th and 19th Centuries* (Franz Steiner Verlag Wiesbaden GMBH, Stuttgart, 1985); Michel Seurat, *L'Etat de Barbarie* (Seuil, Paris, 1989); Patrick Seale, *Asad* (I B Tauris, London, 1988) and *The Struggle for Syria* (Oxford University Press, 1965); Stephen Starr, *Revolt in Syria* (Hurst, London, 2012); Andrew Tabler, *In the Lion's Den* (Lawrence Hill Books, Chicago, 2011);

Nicolaos Van Dam, *The Struggle for Power in Syria* (I B Tauris, London and New York, 2011, first published 1979); Stefan Weber, Damascus, *Ottoman Modernity and Urban Transformation 1808-1918* (2 vols), Proceedings of the Danish Institute in Damascus, 2009; Lisa Wedeen, *Ambiguities of Domination* (University of Chicago Press, 1999); Carsten Wieland, *A Decade of Lost Chances* (Cune Press, Seattle, 2012) and *Syria at Bay* (Hurst, London, 2006); Samar Yazbek, *A Woman in the Crossfire* (Haus Publishing, 2012); Radwan Ziadeh, *Power and Policy in Syria* (I B Tauris, London and New York, 2013); and Eyal Zisser, *Asad's Legacy* (Hurst, London, 2001).

Revolutionary Culture by Robin Yassin-Kassab

Books mentioned include Lisa Wedeen, *Ambiguities of Domination* (University of Chicago Press, 1999); Khaled Khalifa, *In Praise of Hatred* (Doubleday, New York, 2012); and Nihad Sirees, *The Silence and the Roar* (Pushkin Press, London, 2013).

My journalism on the revolution and counter-revolutions is collected at www.qunfuz.com; and examples of revolutionary stamps and a great deal of other material can be seen at http://www.creativememory. org/?cat=27

You can listen to Sameeh Shuqair's 'Ya Heif' here http://www.youtube. com/watch?v=GIObVSytH_w and Da'el is in full song at http://www. youtube.com/watch?v=tsELjr9TQCQ . The 'Top Goon' shows can be viewed at: http://www.youtube.com/playlist?list=PLFC068715C22D0 02C . A promotional video for 'Oxygen' is at https://www.youtube.com/ watch?v=VP7fsiwOgSE and one for "Aneb Biladi' (both with English sub-titles) is at https://www.youtube.com/watch?v=f77XLWNzFMw. A list of photography collectives is at https://www.facebook.com/ lists/444809032274125 and Ibrahim Qashoush leads the crowd here http://www.youtube.com/watch?v=HNauJ8P1fDY

Tammam Azzam's Facebook page is at https://www.facebook.com/ pages/Tammam-Azzam/218202171577341 ; Wissam al-Jazairy's https:// www.facebook.com/lwissamartl and Nabd's Facebook page is at https:// www.facebook.com/nabd.shabab.syria (in Arabic).

Yasser Munif describes the work of the Manbij revolutionary council here http://syrianobserver.com/Features/Features/Manbij+a+Success+Stor y+in+the+Liberated+Areas. See also, Elliot Higgins's highly-regarded blog at http://brown-moses.blogspot.co.uk/

The Revolution's Armed Islamists by Sam Charles Hamad

Patrick Cockburn's article on the Bab al-Hawa crisis is available at: http://www.counterpunch.org/2013/12/16/the-bankruptcy-of-the-wests-syrian-policy/ and Aaron Lund's article on the Islamic Front at: http://carnegieendowment.org/syriaincrisis/?fa=54204
'You can still see their blood', the Human Rights Watch report on the August 2013 massacre of civilians, can be read at: http://www.hrw.org/reports/2013/10/11/you-can-still-see-their-blood Karl Marx's article on the Russian Empire and Turkey can be accessed at https://www.marxists.org/archive/marx/works/1853/07/14.htm.

The Bra in Aleppo by Malu Halasa

For more on Aleppo's lingerie industry, see Malu Halasa and Rana Salam, editors, *The Secret Life of Syrian Lingerie: Intimacy and Design* (Chronicle Books, San Francisco, 2008). For a general history of lingerie, see Karen Bressler, Karoline Newman and Gillian Proctor, *A Century of Lingerie: Revealing the Secrets and Allure of 20th Century Lingerie* (Chartwell Books, Edison, NJ, 1997). And on the history of textiles in Muslim lands, see Patricia Baker, *Islamic Textiles* (British Museum Press, London, 1995). The catalogue of *The 8th International Photography Gathering: Aleppo 2004* by Issa Touma was published by Le Pont Gallery, Aleppo, in 2004.

The Lost Child in Oversized Shoes by Afra Jalabi

The Human Rights Watch report on Syria can be downloaded from: http://www.hrw.org/news/2013/10/03 syria-political-detainees-tortured-killed

Not Even the Basement Escapes by Frederic Gijsel

Michel Foucault's 1967 lecture, 'Of Other Spaces', where he coined the concept of heterotopia, can be found in his collection, *Aesthetics, Method, Epistemology* (Essential Works Vol.2), edited by James D. Faubion (Allen Lane, London, 1999) and in Nicholas Mirzoeff, editor, *The Visual Culture Reader* (Routledge, London, 2012). Khaled Khalifa's *In Praise of Hatred* is available in paperback (Black Swan, London, 2013)

Protecting the Cultural Heritage by Ross Burns

For more detail on the history and archaeology of Syria, see Ross Burns, *Monuments of Syria* (I B Tauris, London, 2009). My website www.monu-mentsofsyria.com provides a pictorial survey of the archaeology of Syria as a visual accompaniment to the book; and my archive of over 80,000 images of archaeological sites is being processed for two database collections: Manar al-Athar at Oxford University (http://www.manar-al-athar. ox.ac.uk); and a website to be maintained by the Near Eastern Archaeological Foundation at the University of Sydney.

The quotes from Jonathan Tubb are from: 'Editorial: Syria's Cultural Heritage' in *Palestine Exploration Quarterly* 145/3 2013: 177–181. The website of the Association for the Protection of Syrian Archaeology (APSA), documenting acts of plunder, is located at: http://www.apsa2011.com; and Unesco's campaign for Safeguarding Syrian Cultural Heritage can be examined at:

http://www.unesco.org/new/en/culture/themes/illicit-traffic-of-cultural-property/emergency-actions/syria/

Old Damascus by Brigid Waddams

For more on old Damascus, see Brigid Keenan and Tom Beddow, *Damascus: Hidden Treasures of the Old City* (Thames and Hudson, London, 2008). The quotes are from: *A Scandalous Life: The Biography of Jane Digby* by Mary S Lovell (Fourth Estate, London, 1998); Freya Stark, *Letters from Syria* (John Murray, London, 1942); Isabel Burton, *The Inner Life of Syria, Palestine, and* the *Holy Land* (London, 1884); Mark Twain, *The Innocents Abroad* (American Publishing Company, Hartford, Conn., 1869); and Ross Burns from *Damascus, A History* (Routledge, London 2005).

Last Word: On Religious Environmentalism by Ehsan Masood

The Environmental Performance Index can be accessed at: http://epi.yale.edu/epi

Lynn White Jr's classic paper, 'The Historical Roots of Our Ecological Crisis' appeared in *Science* 155 1203 1967. Zaheer Baber, *The Science of Empire: Scientific Knowledge, Civilization, and Colonial Rule in India* is published State University of New York Press, New York, 1996.

CONTRIBUTORS

Moniza Alvi is a Pakistani-British poet and writer ● **Itab Azzam** is a Syrian freelance producer and filmmaker currently working in London ● **Ross Burns** is the author of *Monuments of Syria* and *Damascus: A History*; he was Australian Ambassador in Syria and Lebanon from 1984 to 1987 ● **Peter Clark** has translated Syrian fiction, and is the author of many books, including *Marmaduke Pickthall: British Muslim* and *Istanbul; his Damascus Diaries* will be published by Gilgamesh in the autumn of 2014 ● **Yasmin Fedda** is a documentary filmmaker and co-founder of Reel Arts ● **Frederic Gijsel** is an Anthropology graduate from Utrecht University, the Netherlands ● **Daniel Gorman** is a cultural producer and co-founder of Reel Arts ● **Golan Haji** is a Syrian poet, translator and pathologist; his new collection of poetry, *Autumn Here Is Magical and Vast*, was published in Rome, 2013 ● **Malu Halasa**, editor and journalist covering the culture and politics of the Middle East, is the author of *The Secret Life of Syrian Lingerie* and other books ● **Sam Charles Hamad** is an activist and graduate student in history at the University of Edinburgh ● **Amal Hanano** is the pseudonym of Lina Sergie Attar, Syrian American architect and writer ● **Thomas W. Hill** teaches Modern Middle East History at UC Berkeley ● **Afra Jalabi**, a Montreal-based Syrian writer, serves on the Executive Committee of The Day After project, which is engaged in an independent transition planning process for a post-Assad Syria ● **Ehsan Masood** has left *Nature* and *New Scientist* behind but continues his work as a science journalist ● **Maysaloon** writes the blog of that name, and sometimes writes as Shadia Safwan ● **Hania Mourtada** is a Syrian freelance journalist covering the Levant, a production assistant at National Public Radio and a reporter at *Time* magazine ● **Rasha Omran** is a well-known Syrian poet ● **Ruth Padel**, one of the foremost poets of Britain, teaches poetry at Kings College, London; her latest book is *Learning to Make an Oud in Nazareth* ● **Laurens de Rooij** is completing his doctorate in theology and religion at Durham University ● **Zakaria Tamer** is a master of the Arabic very short story ● **Boyd Tonkin**, an award winning journalist, writes for the *Independent* ● **Brigid Waddams**, writer and journalist, wrote *Damascus: Hidden Treasures of the Old City* (as Brigid Keenan), together with photographer Tim Beddow ● **Ella Wind** is an editor at Jadaliyya and a graduate student in Middle East Studies at New York University ● **Robin Yassin-Kassab** has just finished a novel set in the Syrian revolution.